Cont

A Chain
of Hands

By Carol Ryrie Brink

*Buffalo Coat**
Harps in the Wind
Stopover
The Headland
*Strangers in the Forest**
The Twin Cities
Château Saint Barnabé
*Snow in the River**
The Bellini Look
*Four Girls on a Homestead***

*Indicates a Washington State University Press reprint.
**Published by and available from the Latah County Historical Society, Moscow, Idaho.

A Chain of Hands

Carol Ryrie Brink

With a Foreword by Mary E. Reed

Washington State University Press
Pullman, Washington

Published in collaboration with the
Latah County Historical Society
Moscow, Idaho

Washington State University Press, Pullman, Washington 99164-5910

Library of Congress Cataloging-in-Publication Data
Brink, Carol Ryrie, 1895-
    A chain of hands / Carol Ryrie Brink : with a foreword by Mary
E. Reed.
        p.   cm.
    "Published in collaboration with the Latah County Historical Society, Moscow, Idaho."
    Includes bibliographical references.
    ISBN 0-87422-098-X
    1. Brink, Carol Ryrie, 1895-   —Homes and haunts—Idaho—
Moscow. 2. Brink, Carol Ryrie, 1895-   —Biography—Youth.
3. Authors, American—20th century—Biography. 4. Moscow (Idaho)—
Social life and customs. 5. Moscow (Idaho)—Biography.   I. Latah
County Historical Society.   II. Title.
PS3503.R5614Z463   1993
813'.52—dc20   93-6908
    [B]   CIP

Author's Biography

C AROL RYRIE BRINK was born in Moscow, Idaho, in 1895 and spent most of her life there until her junior year in college. Her youthful years spanned the settlement period of rustic one-story, wood-frame buildings lining Main Street to an era of paved roads and automobiles. At a young age her father died of consumption; a crazed gunman murdered her grandfather, one of the town's builders; and her mother committed suicide after an unfortunate second marriage. Carol's maternal grandmother and aunt raised her in their Moscow home.

Brink wrote more than thirty books for both adults and children. Her most acclaimed work, *Caddie Woodlawn,* won the Newbery Medal as the outstanding contribution to children's literature in 1936. It details and synthesizes in fictionalized form the stories her grandmother told her about growing up in Wisconsin. In addition to the Newbery Medal, Brink was honored with the Friends of American Writers Award in 1955, the 1966 National League of

American Pen Women's award for fiction, and an honorary degree of Doctor of Letters from the University of Idaho in 1965.

Brink wrote three stories for children based upon her experiences growing up in Moscow. She also wrote an adult series of novels about her family in and around Moscow: *Buffalo Coat* (1944); *Strangers in the Forest* (1959); and *Snow in the River* (1964). In 1993 the Washington State University Press, in collaboration with the Latah County Historical Society in Moscow, Idaho, reprinted the latter three novels, along with Brink's previously unpublished reminiscences about characters she knew in Moscow, *A Chain of Hands*.

Carol Ryrie Brink died in 1981 in San Diego. Her home town recognized her posthumously with the naming of a building on the University of Idaho campus in her honor and with the naming of the children's wing of the Moscow-Latah County Public Library after her.

Among Brink's contributions to Western American literature are her works about her native state of Idaho. In view of the relatively few Idaho writers of this period, that is of interest in itself. But there are more important considerations for recognizing Brink, especially her portrayal of a West between two eras.

Although many writers concentrate on a colorful pioneer period and the heroic feats of those who plowed virgin ground, opened the first mines, and platted towns, the chronicle of those who followed is certainly equally or more important. These were the people who established the libraries, invested their lives and fortunes in the new communities, and generally created civic life as we recognize it today. Brink's portrayal of the lives and experiences of men and women in an Idaho town during this crucial period of growth and maturing serve as an antidote to numerous works about the wild American frontier. In her three Idaho novels and *A Chain of Hands* she shows us a small town whose citizens had to weigh justice with empathy, who had to learn that the resources of the West were not entirely at their personal disposal, and who discovered that the promise of these new lands was at times ephemeral.

Acknowledgments

IN 1981 I HAD the great pleasure of spending a week with Carol Ryrie Brink in her San Diego home, tape recording hours of conversation about her writing career and her life in Idaho.

I had grown up delighting in Brink's *Caddie Woodlawn*. When I became a historian and began doing volunteer work with the Latah County Historical Society, I discovered that this talented children's author was also an accomplished writer of adult fiction. I was surprised to learn that Brink's three fine adult novels set in Idaho — *Buffalo Coat, Strangers in the Forest,* and *Snow in the River* — had all but been ignored by Idahoans. I found this strange in a state that sometimes overreached for the most tenuous claims to other writers, notably Ezra Pound and Ernest Hemingway, neither of whom wrote about Idaho.

The Idaho Humanities Council awarded a grant to the Historical Society that allowed me to undertake a project to bring greater attention to the Idaho works of Brink. Thus, I found myself in that summer of 1981 spending delightful days in her company, including a fine picnic overlooking the Pacific Ocean.

During the course of our conversations Brink mentioned to me that she had one remaining unpublished manuscript, "A Chain of Hands," a work of reminiscences about some of the people she knew while growing up in Moscow, many of whom would — in fictionalized form — play roles in her works for children and adults. The Latah County Historical Society had already published one of Brink's works, *Four Girls on a Homestead,* and had reprinted *Buffalo Coat.* So I asked and received permission for the Society to publish "A Chain of Hands."

When I returned to the Palouse I received a letter from one of Brink's friends letting me know that Carol had had a sudden heart attack. She died a month after we met, although she had been in fine health and excellent spirits at the time of our conversations, and had looked forward to visiting Moscow again.

Over the course of the decade following her death, Society volunteers worked "A Chain of Hands" into publishable form, retaining the language as Brink had written it, but copyediting it and entering the manuscript onto computer disk. However, as publication costs continued to escalate, it became apparent that the Society would not be able to produce "Chain" in the quality it deserved without assistance. So we sought a collaboration with the Washington State University Press.

In the 1980s the Press and Society had collaborated in the publication of two other successful books, and in 1992 agreed to another collaborative venture, an ambitious project to produce four works by Carol Ryrie Brink: this first edition of *A Chain of Hands,* as well as reprints of her three adult novels set in Idaho.

This publication would not have been possible without the dedicated efforts over many years of two longtime friends of the Society who also know and appreciate Brink's works, Carolyn Gravelle and Kathleen Probasco. They kept this project alive when it appeared we might have to abandon publication plans, and we at the Society appreciate all they have done.

Special thanks are due to the Society's publications committee and board of trustees for their foresight in recognizing the importance of regional publishing in general and Brink's work specifically. I wish to especially thank Bert Cross of the publications committee, who supported this project when others became discouraged. And I owe Jim Maguire my warm thanks for including a monograph on Carol Brink in the prestigious Western Writers Series published by Boise State University Press, and for allowing us to use the biographical section in the foreword that follows.

The Brink publication venture would not have been possible without the kind and generous assistance of the Brink family, and we are indebted to Carol's son David and daughter Nora Brink Hunter for their encouragement and help. And this project was in many ways undertaken in Carol Brink's memory. Her last work has come out posthumously, but I think she would have been pleased.

At the WSU Press I would like to thank director Thomas Sanders and assistant director Mary Read for understanding how important the Brink works are as regional literature. The Press deserves much credit for recognizing in this, and numerous other projects, that high-quality "local" history is simply high-quality history. Its continuing policy of publishing important works on the history and culture of communities and people throughout eastern Washington and northern Idaho is commendable and of immeasurable value to all of us who labor in the fields of local and state history.

I would also like to thank other members of the Press staff: editor Keith Petersen, who is in many ways responsible for bringing this project to fruition; editors Glen Lindeman, Jean Taylor, and John Sutherland; designer Dave Hoyt; and marketing and promotions coordinator Vida Hatley, a strong proponent of publishing the Brink books from the very beginning.

Mary E. Reed
Latah County Historical Society
Moscow, Idaho

Foreword

FOR A GIFTED STORYTELLER with the ability to pluck the extraordinary from the ordinary, the occasion of Carol Ryrie Brink's birth would give her the opportunity to introduce herself into a particular place and time. Her life tentatively began on December 28, 1895. She grew up hearing the story of that winter evening from her grandmother so often that it became her own. Her grandfather, Dr. William W. Watkins, arrived at the Ryrie house on a sleigh pulled through the snow by his high-stepping horse. As the doctor pumped the baby's small arms up and down and blew his tobacco-scented breath into the cold, still body, an anxious father and exhausted mother waited to hear the thin wail. As Brink tells in her reminiscences, "I gave a sharp cry to begin what has been a marvelous and rewarding journey, a thing too precious to be minimized: my lovely life" *(Chain, 4)*.

The world she entered was a modest house in Moscow, Idaho, the seat of a rural county in the northern part of the state. It boasted the distinction of having the state university, and although isolated, Moscow was firmly connected with the outside world by the new railroad. Living in Moscow until her junior year at the University of Idaho gave Brink an intimate knowledge of this crucial time of development. Her youthful years spanned the settlement period of rustic one-story, wood-frame buildings lining Main Street to an era of paved roads and automobiles. In between, the pace was measured by foot or horseback, Main Street being the center of business and commerce, with social and cultural life firmly clinging to church and civic clubs.

Brink entered this small-town Western scene as the youngest member of a well-respected family. William W. Watkins was a popular physician with a domineering personality who, as his granddaughter remembered, people either liked or disliked. As Brink describes him, "He was a big man with a dark handle-bar moustache. He was used to getting what he wanted. In his photographs he has a fierce and angry look. . . . Proud, confident, dynamic, single-purposed. . ."

(Chain, 4, 6). After practicing medicine in Missouri and Kansas, he moved his family to Moscow in 1887.

In Moscow Dr. Watkins became a pillar of the community, distinguishing himself by helping to secure the state university and serving as regent for the school. He became prominent in the Masons, owned property, and was, in short, symbolic of the new Western opportunist.

The other dominant male figures in Brink's early life were her father, Alexander Ryrie, and his brother Donald. Four of these Scottish brothers came to Moscow; one returned to Scotland. The gentle-natured Alexander worked for a large Scottish life insurance firm. He also served as mayor, surveyed the city streets, and taught Sunday School at the Presbyterian Church. The more aggressive Donald speculated in real estate and irrigation projects and lived a faster pace. A third brother, Henry, was considerably more carefree and less successful. This variety of avuncular personalities assuredly helped form Carol Brink's healthy attitude toward men and marriage.

Brink's mother, Henrietta, was a beautiful and emotional woman and a gifted musician but – as her daughter remembered – not very interested in being a mother. Brink admitted that at the time of her mother's death she possessed few memories of this mysterious woman. As she grew older, Brink became convinced her mother had little love for her. In fact, the emotional ties between mother and daughter were so lacking that Brink poignantly recounts one instance when a strange young woman gave her a warmth and tenderness she had sought but had not received from her own mother. In later years she could fit this isolated piece into a wider perspective. For, "though my mother must have fondled me and taken me upon her lap or held me in her arms or even lain beside me on a bed a great many times in the eight years we were together, I cannot remember one of them. There must have been in her embrace something perfunctory and unfelt; a duty done toward a little, homely child who did not occupy the center of her heart" *(Chain,* 23). Fortunately for her writing career, she was able to overcome this emotional deprivation.

Brink's grandmother, Caroline Watkins, amply provided the maternal bond. Prevented by her parents from marrying her first love, she married the young doctor. Of their six children, three died in infancy. At her husband's death she found herself with a lapsed insurance policy, rundown property, a stack of unpaid bills, and a grandchild to rear. Fortunately she possessed the inner resources that allowed her to sustain her losses and passed on to the young Brink the lessons not only of accepting life as it came but also of stability, security, wisdom, and good sense. Her influences shaped Brink's life and writing into an optimistic and realistic harmony. Brink admits that her grandmother crept into nearly every book she wrote, sometimes as the chief character, sometimes with a minor part, and sometimes merely by imbuing the book with her spirit *(Chain,* 32).

Caroline Watkins also represented a romantic spirit because of her vivid memories of a childhood on the Wisconsin frontier. Her stories about her childhood greatly influenced the genesis of Brink's writing career, for they gave the child a sense of continuity with the past. Gram's life offered a wonderful contrast between her childhood—which Brink immortalized in *Caddie Woodlawn* in the tomboy who befriended the Indians and scandalized the circuit rider—and the quiet old woman who seldom left the house, whose interests were not broad, and whose opinions were not unusual.

Brink's aunts, Elsie and Winifred, also influenced her life and works. Elsie was a complicated person who, frustrated by her father's refusal to let her become a nurse, lived at home most of her adult life. After Brink's mother died, Elsie took over Carol's upbringing with an engulfing devotion. This affection and dedication threatened to possess Brink, but fortunately she was able to nourish a small seed of individuality that kept her "from being completely her thing." It was Aunt Elsie who shared the young Carol's bedroom, making her room comfortable and placing a protective arm around her in the bed they shared. Eventually Brink asserted her independence and Aunt Elsie moved downstairs, greatly hurt by this act of rebellion from her niece *(Chain,* 33-36).

Elsie also provided a lesson in the complexities of women "caught between the pruderies of Victoria and the freer thinking of the Edwardians." Although she had an unbridled tongue and frequently made indiscreet, shocking remarks, inside she was "completely virginal," and "horrified by license in other people" *(Chain,* 101).

Winifred proved a disruptive element, a wild card. Brink admits she spent most of her life disliking Aunt Win. Like Henrietta, Winifred was temperamental and a talented musician, but unlike her older sister she was lazy, self-centered, and lacking in responsibility. Her father's favorite, at the time of his death Winifred was "a little red-haired girl of twelve" prepared to violently rebel against her mother. Having witnessed many painful scenes between Winifred, Elsie, and Caroline, Brink determined to avoid this chaos in her own life.

When Winifred was sixteen she eloped with a man twice her age. Returning for a brief period to Moscow, Winifred found an appropriate outlet for her great vitality by becoming the accompanist for the local movie house. When she tired of this occupation she left her husband and two sons to run away with a handsome doctor. She left her two young boys in the capable hands of Caroline Watkins. Although communications from Winifred, who changed her name to Wanda, were scarce, "they nearly always ended on the same note: a plea for money" *(Chain,* 41).

Winifred died in poverty, but her influence persisted in Brink's novels. The author's initial sense of outrage mellowed into acceptance and an attempt to understand the complexities of this restless woman. This was an important healing process because it allowed Brink to use Winifred's character in many novels without moralizing or creating a stereotype.

The series of events which destroyed Brink's secure childhood world spanned a brief three years from her fifth to her eighth year. Alexander Ryrie died of consumption in July 1900. The next year, on August 4, 1901, a crazed gunman murdered William Watkins. Although Brink was not as emotionally attached to her grandfather as to her grandmother, his death brought the reality of violence into her early life. Because she grew up with the accounts of the murder and of the killer's death after a two-hour gun battle with a posse, Brink realized how such incidents become an integral part of a town's communal memory. The incident posed questions of justice and mob action in a small Western town, questions that she would explore in *Buffalo Coat.*

These deaths were followed by one of greater personal consequence. After Alexander's death Henrietta married Nat Brown, the son of a prominent timber buyer. Brown had made some fast, lucrative deals with the Weyerhaeuser timber concern and he was, according to Brink, more interested in social pleasures than family responsibilities, particularly those concerning his shy and plain stepdaughter. In *Snow in the River,* Brink admits a distaste for this man, an aversion which increased rather than diminished with time *(Snow,* 167). During this period Brink found solace in her grandmother's house. Although the memory of her stepfather was one of distaste, she admitted that "It must be difficult for a man to love a former husband's child, especially if that child is silent and resentful" *(Snow,* 177). Henrietta and Nat Brown became part of Moscow's faster social set, and Brink describes him as a man who drank too much, used profanity, and fought with her mother.

The marriage added another layer of gossip onto the Watkins household. Henrietta's suicide in 1904 was the outcome of this desperate unhappiness, leaving Carol an orphan and in the care of her grandmother and her spinster aunt. No one told Brink the circumstances of her mother's death until she was eighteen or nineteen; by then it was neither a shock nor a surprise, "but only a rude bringing into the open of what had been tacitly understood" *(Chain,* 21). In the description of the chilling numbness she felt at her mother's death—one of Brink's best-written passages—she describes herself as a cold and quiet little girl, dry eyed and grim *(Snow,* 189-90).

After the suicide, Donald Ryrie asked the three Watkins women to come to Spokane and keep house for him. For Brink, it was an idyllic existence because Ryrie enjoyed buying her expensive gifts and showing her off to his friends. This happy interlude abruptly ended when he remarried. The three women moved back to Moscow to the large Watkins home, but there they had to face another scandal involving Donald's bankruptcy.

With the abrupt changes in their economic and social situation, the Watkins family entered "the next level of caste, the unsung middle class who attended to business but rarely went out socially" *(Chain,* 76). Yet the experience of being an orphan and often lonely had a positive influence on Brink's creativity. The quiet of her grandmother's house trained her to create her own amusements. The childhood hours spent painting, drawing, reading, and riding the Idaho countryside inspired her determination to write and illustrate her own books.

Although Brink received only a modest inheritance from her father, it provided sufficient funds to see her through college. It also became an important emotional link to her father. She grew up with "the confidence of a person of independent means. A generous allowance was doled out to me every week, and I knew that it came from my own money and that more was in the bank" *(Chain,* 73).

Being a precocious child, Brink was aware that their family was different from others in Moscow, that something terrible and unspeakable had happened. Under these circumstances, her ability to face the world cheerfully was fortunate if not remarkable. Instead of being consumed with self-pity and fear she concentrated on developing her inner resources. Her grandmother proved a valuable ally in this process. Gram passed along her innate storytelling abilities to her granddaughter.

Brink and her future husband, Raymond, first met in 1909 when he, only nineteen years old, arrived in Moscow to teach at the university's prep school. He rented a spare room at the Watkins's large house and befriended the thirteen-year-old Carol. A quiet young man, he had progressed rapidly and successfully through school without time for frivolity because he was too young to participate in his classmates' social life. But "Blinky," as Raymond was nicknamed, became a member of the neighborhood bunch that included Caroline and Elsie Watkins and other neighbors. The age difference between Carol and Raymond may have delayed their ultimate attachment and marriage, but these years gave them an opportunity to become good friends. Raymond tutored Carol in mathematics and they invented elaborate codes allowing them to communicate "shy and pleasant things," safe enough for Elsie's scrutiny *(Chain,* 181).

Although Caroline Watkins approved of Raymond, Elsie became alarmed that her niece was slipping away from her. She was furious when Raymond confided at the end of his school term that he intended to marry Carol when she was older. After a summer of exchanging letters, Raymond returned to Moscow but took a room elsewhere because Elsie banned him from the Watkins house. Although the year began with an emotional separation between the couple, it ended with an understanding. The next year Raymond left to complete his studies at Harvard, and their relationship continued through letters.

After Raymond left Moscow, Elsie persuaded the family to move to Portland, Oregon, for Brink's last two years of high school in the Portland Academy. Stricken with homesickness, Brink lived in her aunt and grandmother's Portland apartment instead of boarding at the school. She took comfort in her diary and Raymond's faithful letters, and on Valentine's Day Raymond sent her the usual bouquet of pink carnations. Elsie was silent, but a few days later Brink found a letter from Elsie in her diary demanding that she end her relationship with him. Devastated by this intrusion into her private life, she felt she could never forgive her aunt, who was asking her "to give up one of the dear and human connections that I still had with the world." Still, she complied, sinking into a terrible depression which she remembers as the lowest spot in her life, and "I was just sixteen" *(Chain,* 184).

The next year Brink returned alone to the Portland Academy. As life became brighter, she resolved to resume her correspondence with Raymond after telling her aunt of her intention during the Christmas holidays *(Chain,* 185). This act of defiance finally released her from her aunt's domination. During the year she also conquered a debilitating shyness. When the school magazine printed one of her articles she blossomed under the attention of the editor and the admiration of her colleagues. With a new self-confidence she returned to Moscow and enrolled at the University of Idaho.

Her home town college was her second choice to Wellesley, but that school was beyond the means of her father's legacy. She joined a sorority and enthusiastically participated in college society. Editor of the society page of the school newspaper, she also wrote skits for the class plays. After three years she felt a need to expand her knowledge of the world, so she completed her senior year at the University of California in Berkeley with a close friend from the University of Idaho, Nora Ashton. At Berkeley, Carol became engaged twice while Raymond traveled to France on a fellowship and had romances with two other girls. Their next meeting occurred that fall when he made a special trip to resume the courtship, and the following Christmas he proposed. Her engagement to Raymond foreshadowed a break with Moscow and Idaho that would be more complete than she had imagined or desired *(Chain,* 186-187). Because Elsie had married the previous year, Brink hoped that she could be married in her grandmother's house, but Elsie bluntly forbade it. Out of a misguided sense of helping her niece or perhaps motivated by jealousy, she castigated Carol for jeopardizing a potential writing career with a premature marriage. Devastated by this petty decision, Brink left Moscow to be married at the Brinks' cabin at a Wisconsin lake. This time it was Elsie who cried and Brink who was happy to be done with the old life and start making a new one. That beginning flourished in the warm and wide circle of her new family. Built on a long-nurtured friendship, mutual tastes, and respect, the Brinks' marriage was successful. With the happiness and fulfillment of her adult years, Carol's bitterness over her aunt's pettiness disappeared.

Carol and Raymond's lives evolved smoothly. He taught at the University of Minnesota for the next forty years while Carol enjoyed her role as a faculty wife, although she neglected her social duties for her family and writing. She joined the Faculty Women's Club and initiated a writers' section. Later she taught creative writing at Hamline University in St. Paul, Minnesota. The Brinks' habits were mutually well-suited; both had careers that focused on writing, and there were always two desks at home and in hotels during their travels. Raymond also proved to be a good editor and critic of Carol's works.

The pleasures of marriage widened with the birth of two children, David and Nora, in 1919 and 1926. Her husband's numerous sabbaticals and vacations in Europe became another enriching experience, adding to her repertoire of material for her books. But she never became a writer alienated or exiled from her roots. Her writing career began in a modest manner with numerous stories published in children's magazines. She had not anticipated writing juvenile fiction but was inspired to do so by her children. Writing was a compulsion, but to a woman who put family responsibilities foremost this often meant writing on the end of the ironing board or the kitchen table when the children were in bed or in school. Her rigorous schedule of writing each morning and leaving the afternoons free for family and personal affairs provided a balance that well suited Brink.

Macmillan published Brink's first children's book, *Anything Can Happen on the River,* in 1934. But winning the Newbery Medal for the outstanding work in children's literature in 1936 for *Caddie Woodlawn* gave her the self-confidence to continue writing. Along with giving her immediate recognition as a serious writer, it provided money for household help, freeing her to begin work on her adult novels. Her relationship to Macmillan was mutually beneficial. Except for five juvenile books and a Gothic romance she wrote "just for fun," Macmillan published all her works and editors there encouraged her writing career. One exception was her last manuscript, "A Chain of Hands," written in the 1970s, which they rejected. By then Brink had a new editor at Macmillan and the relationship that had begun in the 1930s ended.

In addition to receiving the Newbery Medal in 1936, Brink was honored with the Friends of American Writers Award in 1955 and an honorary degree of Doctor of Letters from the University of Idaho in 1965. In 1966 the National League of American Pen Women gave her its award for fiction. In the 1980s her reputation enjoyed a renaissance in her home town. When the Moscow Public Library expanded, it dedicated the renovated, original wing as the Carol Ryrie Brink Children's Room. The University of Idaho also acknowledged one of its most notable alums by naming a building Carol Ryrie Brink Hall.

For a year after Raymond's retirement the Brinks lived in Florida, where he taught at the University of Coral Gables. Not liking the climate, they moved to La Jolla, California. When Raymond died in 1976 Carol moved to Wesley Palms, a retirement community in San Diego. After a career of twenty-seven books for children and adults, Brink turned to poetry, painting, and spending time with friends to fill out her remaining years.

Brink was honest about her career and her stature as a writer. She candidly admitted she had been lucky enough to have a small success in her career, and although she dreamt of becoming a great writer, she settled for less. She avoided literary circles and celebrities. Having been snubbed herself, she resolved to be gracious to her own fans and fellow writers (Brink, interview with the author, 1981).

Near the end of her life Brink expressed confidence that she had accomplished all that she had wanted as a writer. There were no unfinished books—with the exception of the yet-unpublished "A Chain of Hands"—no great undone projects, no unhealed wounds. The things that needed to be said were written "in the burning days when I was young." In 1981 she sensed that her last project to write about her experiences in Scotland might never be finished and would probably not find a publisher *(Chain,* 86; interview with the author, 1981). She died in August of that year, full of kindness, vigor, and a strong attachment to her Idaho roots.

Among Brink's contributions to Western American literature are the works about her native state of Idaho. The three adult books set in the Moscow area are *Buffalo Coat, Strangers in the Forest,* and *Snow in the River.* She also wrote three books for children that draw upon her Idaho childhood experiences: *All Over Town, Louly,* and *Two Are Better Than One.* In the 1970s, at the request of the Latah County Historical Society in Moscow, Brink wrote a reminiscence of a summer spent at her aunt's homestead in the white pine forests northeast of the city, *Four Girls on a Homestead.* In view of the relatively few Idaho writers of this period, this body of work is of itself significant. But there are more important considerations. For one, Brink portrays a West between two eras, when towns like Moscow accelerated toward becoming replicas of any small American town. This was the town-building period when women's groups brought to maturity churches and schools, libraries, parks, literary societies, and all the cultural developments of small-town life. It is an aspect of the history of the American West that has only recently begun receiving deserved attention from historians—who can learn a considerable amount from an author like Brink.

Brink also brought to her writing an interpretation of her time period and her social class. She embodies a middle-class restraint of the 1940s and 1950s—when the bulk of her work was written—that avoided revealing personal hostility, bitterness, or alienation. Yet she was not prudish. She was able to weigh the values of respectable society with that same society's impulse to stifle and condemn the nonconformist. Her own social descent from being the mayor's daughter to becoming an orphan gave her a penetrating insight and empathy. She was a non-judgmental champion of decency while retaining a fascination with the daring, impatient, and rebellious women who wanted more than a good marriage and children. In Brink's fiction they are neither scorned nor ridiculed, but neither are they accepted. As she admitted in an interview, writing about her mother in *Snow in the River* was therapeutic because it let her express the anguish she felt from her mother's death and because it allowed her to rid herself of some things that had bothered her all her life (interview with the author). Nonetheless, this novel, like her life, avoided exploiting the personal events.

When *Buffalo Coat* appeared in 1944, Carol Brink was surprised at the commotion it created in Moscow as residents tried to unravel the fiction from the facts. Despite that flurry of excitement, Moscow and Idaho seemed to forget their native author during subsequent years. In 1980 the Latah County Historical Society initiated a long-term project to revitalize interest in her life and career among Idaho residents. The Society's staff gave lectures throughout the state on the author, developed museum exhibits, extensively interviewed Brink and made these oral history tapes available to researchers, and hosted a writers' conference in her honor. In 1991 Boise State University published *Carol Ryrie Brink* as part of its Western Writers Series. This effort to gain recognition is now culminating in a collaborative project between the Historical Society and the Washington State University Press. The publication of the three Idaho novels and the collection of reminiscences, *A Chain of Hands,* will help insure Brink's permanent place in Idaho and Northwest literature. The appearance of these important works near the one hundredth anniversary of her birth is a significant and appropriate tribute to this Idaho author of universal appeal.

MARY E. REED
Latah County Historical Society
Moscow, Idaho
March, 1993

1

First Hands

IN MICHELANGELO'S PAINTING of the creation, God's finger touches Adam's in the first awakening of life. The figures are casual, relaxed. It is not an electric moment; it is a moment of reaching and giving and receiving. So we all reach out to each other and give and receive. I like to think that the touch of life continues from the deep, dark origin of man forward into the deep, dark future. I touch another human being; but behind me was my mother's touch and all of those she touched; and behind her and behind her and behind her all the countless millions of seeking hands that touched, transmitting the mystery of a shared experience. The faces are lost in forgetfulness; only the hands seem to go on: a living chain.

I suppose I should be sorry that I have touched so few celebrities in my lifetime. I have no famous names to drop. But then this book need not be written if the people I touched had written their own histories or carved their own monuments. Those I remember best are unimportant people. When I have stopped remembering them, they will cease to exist in this world. So I must write in order to save a few of the faces that belong to a few of the hands in the endless chain of touch. The hands not only touch, they reach and implore. "Give me a little extra span of life. Take *me!* Take *me!*"

There are so many reaching hands and I can only say, "I can't take all of you. I must pick and choose. And I am getting old. My memory may be faulty. But I'll give the few of you what truth I have."

Mentally I go back and walk again the familiar streets of my childhood, dusty in summer, deep with mud and slush in winter and spring. I walk the high board sidewalks under which hornets used to build their nests and fly out angrily to sting unwary children. I go in and out of vanished buildings, ride my pony between wheat fields and dusty hedges of long-lost wild roses, hear meadowlarks like chimes on lonely fence posts and distant church bells like flying birds. I see the tall Lombardy poplars and smell the keen scent of wet, new lumber or rotting leaves. I see the blue mountains beyond the yellow wheat fields.

I was born in a small north Idaho town, and my first five years were spent in a natural environment of father, mother, home and security. On the edge of our pleasant nest hovered a maternal grandmother and grandfather and an unmarried aunt. When I was five, my father died of consumption, a dread disease for which old cookbooks prescribed a medication of powdered charcoal, honey and port wine. The most modern remedy in his day was to get to Arizona and sit in the sun. He died on the way to Arizona. There followed three years, which seem much longer in retrospect, of insecurity and turbulence. My grandfather met a violent death, and my mother, so recently widowed, made a disastrous marriage. She built a large house next to my grandmother's, and she was so terribly unhappy in it that she saw no clear way of continuing to remain alive. During this period I often felt unwanted and unloved. There was one escape for me — my grandmother's house next door.[1]

After my mother's death I went to live permanently with my grandmother and aunt. There I began a long, serene plateau of existence which continued until my senior year in college, at which time I broke home ties, went away to finish my education in a new environment, and was married to begin a happy life of my own.

Within this chronological framework my unimportant people must fit themselves. They were the first newsbearers who brought me information from a world outside myself. They were the first hands I touched.

2

Grandfather

I WAS THERE in the night of December 28, 1895, but the vivid and detailed mental picture which I have of my own birth comes from my grandmother's eye-witness account rather than from any precocity of my own. She was always a good storyteller and she stocked my receptive mind with an abundance of lively pictures which remain as real to me as the things I saw myself.

So now I see my father struggling through one of those deep, wet blizzards that deposit layer upon layer of heavy snow on the winter mountains of northern Idaho. He is hurrying to tell my grandfather that my mother has begun her labor. My grandfather is a doctor, probably the chief one at the time in this small pioneer town. He lives only four blocks away from my parents, but the blocks are long and they wander up and down hill. My grandfather is not a man who likes to wait. He likes to arrive smartly behind a high-stepping horse with a musical jingling of bells. When he hears that his daughter needs him, he goes to the barn and hitches the horse to the sleigh while my grandmother gathers together the things they will need.[2]

My parents lived in a little pink house with a large, round front window decorated with a border of colored glass. There was a large yard surrounded by a pink picket fence which was now lost in drifting snow. The interior of the house was lit by coal-oil lamps, and fires were going briskly in the kitchen range and baseburner.

My father is not mentioned again in the account, so I imagine him plodding back the way he came, quiet on the surface in his habitual Scotch reserve, but unnaturally apprehensive from within. My grandmother Watkins and my Scotch father, although they were related only by marriage, shared many of the same characteristics: stability, patience, kindness, and a calm approach to any emergency.

But a first child and an emotional, beautiful, high-strung wife crying out in unwanted pain must have been enough to unsettle the sturdiest Scotsman. It must have been a relief to him to turn things over to the doctor, especially to the father who was so much like his daughter. My mother's flashing dark eyes, her charm, her emotional instability were all inherited from my grandfather Watkins.

My mother was small-boned and delicately formed. I have a trunk full of her dresses, so pretty and lacy and ruffled and gaily colored. But so small. I cannot get them across my broader shoulders, and at the time of my birth she was eight years younger than when these dresses were made. She was not a woman made for child birth. Perhaps if I had been a small-boned baby...but I had happened to catch the sturdy Scotch peasant genes, and I did not arrive easily. The water boiled and was pushed to the back of the stove; the linens warmed before the fire. All through the night the dreadful struggle to bring forth a child went on in the little bedroom of the pink house. When finally I was born into the world, I had no cry of triumph left in me. "Stillborn!" my grandmother whispered. I was the first grandchild, and they had had high hopes. (But now comes the heroic part of the tale, the part I used to love to hear.)

My grandfather took me up and blew into my lungs. He was a big man with a dark handle-bar moustache. He was used to getting what he wanted. In his photographs he has a fierce and angry look. He pumped my small arms up and down, then filled my lungs with his warm, vital breath. He was a great cigar smoker so the breath was probably scented with tobacco. But finally I began to breathe and squirm. I gave a sharp cry to begin what has been a marvelous and rewarding journey, a thing too precious to be minimized: my lovely life. I have always been grateful to my grandfather. He died when I was five and I have few first-hand recollections of him, but this is enough. He gave me my life even more surely than my parents did, and I have enjoyed it more than I can ever tell.

It is ironical that out of eight children of his own, he was able to save only three; those three, girls. I think he had a healthy masculine scorn of women, since his three little sons died before they were three years old. I have their pictures, handsome little boys, all looking forward to a good life, with one mounted on a hobby horse.

My grandfather was a respected and competent physician for his day, but even the best of doctors had not learned to cope with diphtheria, scarlet fever, or any of the other childhood scourges that have so nearly been eradicated today.

Although I was another girl, he thought well enough of me to enter my name in red ink in the case book where he recorded births, and after the usual vital statistics, he put in parentheses, "My first grandchild!" I am also grateful to him for that exclamation point.

William Woodbury Watkins was born in Warner, New Hampshire, on August 3, 1846. His father was of Welsh descent. His mother was a cousin of Jacob and John C. Abbott, both best-selling authors of their day. Lyman Abbott, the celebrated New England preacher, was his second cousin; and Emma Abbott, the singer, a close connection. Phoebe, his mother, died when he was quite small and he was reared by some elder sisters. His father was unable or unwilling to give him financial assistance with his education so he never went to high school. Somehow he drifted South, and there a man named Duke became very much interested in him and financed his medical education. The St. Louis Medical University took him in without high school credits. He was duly graduated and later served for a time on the faculty there as a lecturer on women's and children's diseases.

Some years after my grandfather's death, Mr. Duke came to visit my grandmother. He was a quiet, courtly Southern gentleman with gray hair, and to me he always seemed a mysterious figure. After several days with us he still remained a mystery, but he had apparently had a sincere interest in and feeling for my grandfather. He seemed wealthy in a quiet and unostentatious way, but we never knew whether he belonged to the tobacco Dukes or really who he was.

In St. Louis my grandfather met Caroline Augusta Woodhouse and asked her to marry him. She was sitting on the side porch of her house shelling peas into a pan when he asked her to marry him. She was just recovering from a deeply felt love affair with a young man who drank too much and of whom her parents disapproved. She said, "Yes." When they came to tell her of her husband's death on August 4, 1901, she was sitting on the side porch of her house in Idaho shelling peas into a pan for his Sunday dinner.

After practicing medicine in several towns in Missouri and Kansas, he took his family to Moscow, Idaho, in August 1887. August seems to have been his month of destiny. "Leo, born to be king," says the horoscope. "The sun is Leo's ruler, and you are the sun's own people – proud, confident, dynamic, single-purposed. Your generosity and warmth reach all. Lucky day is Sunday." But he was shot on Sunday; however, proud, confident, dynamic, single-purposed do describe him. He fought to get the state university for his town, and he served as regent from 1893 to 1895. He gave the Watkins Medal for Oratory.[3] He was the first president of the Idaho State Medical Association in 1893-94. And he drove all over the countryside in his buffalo-hide coat, delivering babies and naming them after himself or his daughters. People adored him or they hated him. There was no halfway ground. He insisted on getting the biggest bell in town for the Presbyterian Church that was across the street from his home, and then it nearly drove him crazy whenever its booming woke him up on Sunday morning. He insisted that Grandma get the recipe for some delicious cookies that had been given him by one of his admiring patients, and when Grandma made them from the recipe, he said they weren't the same.

"But, Doctor," Grandma said, "I used all of the same ingredients."

"Too bad," he said. "Yours are round and hers were square."

I have told elsewhere of the manner of my grandfather's death, and, although the account appears in a book of fiction, it is essentially true.[4]

On August 4, 1901, the day after his fifty-fifth birthday, Dr. Watkins was driving to his office in his phaeton after making a sick call with a little girl on Orchard Street. It was 9:30 in the morning of a hot summer day and the first bells had rung for church in our town of many bells. The second bells never rang because a crazed farmer, named William Steffens, rode into town on horseback with a list in his pocket of prominent citizens and ammunition for his pistol. My grandfather was the first man he met who was on his list. He met the phaeton at a street intersection and put his horse in the way of the doctor's horse.

"Hello, Doctor," he called, and my grandfather stopped the horse and leaned forward to speak to him. He knew Steffen as a fellow

Mason, but a man with a bad reputation for violence and unbridled cruelty. A few months earlier the doctor had gone out to Steffens's farm at the behest of other Masons to reason with the forty-year-old farmer over the reported beating and mistreating of his mother. Steffens was eventually brought into court by the sheriff and publicly reprimanded. As the doctor leaned forward to speak, Steffens shot and killed him with the first bullet. He shot again and again before he whirled his horse and rode on into town.

My grandfather's mare was frightened into a gallop, but she only knew one way to go without guidance. She galloped to the familiar office and drew up quietly at the hitching post with her dead master fallen forward across the reins.

Then began a siege of terror that was new to the town. It was something out of the old West with which we are all too familiar today through the flimsy medium of movies and TV. In those days it did not happen often; but it was real, not make-believe. Steffens rode up and down the streets looking for the victims he had put upon his list. One was out of town, some were safely in their houses, but he wounded a prominent merchant and several others. One of these, Deputy Sheriff George Cool, later died of his wounds. People were too terrified and disorganized to stop a man who was made to show his power for destruction. But at last a sheriff's bullet broke the leg of Steffens's horse, and the farmer had to flee on foot to his house just out of town on the road to the cemetery. At first none dared follow him.[5]

The second bells for church did not ring that Sunday morning, but the hardware store owners unlocked their doors and gave out guns and ammunition to the men of the town. The posse, cautious but fortified by outrage, followed the farmer out to this home and crawled through the wheat, surrounding his house. He returned their shots from the upper windows, and a pitched battle went on for nearly two hours. At last Steffens's mother came out and called, "Don't shoot anymore. My son is dead."

None knew who shot him. It was like a firing squad.

I remember the house as it looked when I was a child. It stood up, narrow and stark, perpendicular as a city dwelling and surrounded by flat yellow wheat fields. It was unpainted and weathered, and I could still see the bullet holes in it.

Many people from all walks of life in our community crowded the church at my grandfather's funeral. There were the curious, the devoted patients, the Masons, the business associates, the old, and the young. One little girl walked miles from the country to lay a bunch of wilting wild flowers on his coffin.

Violence is not readily forgotten. Worthier men have been lost sight of, but, because of the manner of his death, my grandfather has become a part of the history of the town. People still speak of him and show his grave.

3

Lena

THEY USED TO tell me that the first words I learned to speak were in Swedish perhaps because one of the first persons I remember outside my immediate family was Lena, the Swedish hired girl. Lena was a tall, raw-boned girl from a neighboring farm who must have been very young; for, when I saw her sixty years later, she seemed no older than I was. She was a part of my surrounds, like the brick walk at the front of the house where the ants labored among the grasses that had sprung up between the bricks, like the slanting cellar door at the back where I used to slide and get my buttocks full of splinters, like the gate that I used to untie when I wanted to run away to my grandmother's.

In those days the Swedish farm daughters usually went to work in town. It was their education. They were wholesome, sturdy girls, used to hard work and eager to learn what they could from the housewives of town and to make a little dowry money at the same time. They grew up to be the backbone of our society; their sons became lawyers or doctors or good, Christian businessmen.

But often, under the practical surface, these girls had a romantic side — a yearning for something more exciting than feeding the pigs and washing up the dishes. My grandmother used to tell about one of her Swedish hired girls who consulted a fortune teller. The fortune teller told her that she would take a long journey and find a husband. It was a stock prediction that might be told to any female customer. But Christiana came back and told my grandmother that she was sorry but she had to quit her job.

"Aren't you happy here, Christiana?" Grandmother asked.

"Oh, ja, I like it here. But now dis lady tell me I gotta go. I go back to Sweden and I get a husband."

In vain my grandmother argued that the fortune teller did not mean that she was to quit her job and leave at once, but nothing would dissuade her. She left for Sweden as soon as she could pack, and in due course she came back with a husband. She believed her fortune and she made it a reality.

I am sure that Lena had the same credulous belief in the romantic life. She had seen the movies and she had her own liberal ideas of how the famous lived. To her I became one of the famous, and what she remembered of me was overlaid with what she imagined a California writer's life to be. I was still her child, her baby girl, but now I had become a celebrity. When I returned to my old college to receive an honorary degree, she read about it in the newspaper and she was the first person who came to call on me at the hotel.[6]

My husband and I had had a long, dusty automobile trip, so one of the first things I did, when I reached the hotel, was to take a shower and wash my hair. I was blissfully showering when there came a knocking on the hotel room door. My husband answered it. A tall, elderly woman rushed in.

"Vere is my Carol? My little baby girl?" she cried.

My husband was puzzled, but he allowed her to come in. Eventually I emerged in a dressing gown and slippers with a towel wrapped around my head. Lena folded me to her bosom. She held me at arm's length and looked at me. Again I was enfolded and kissed. She did not seem to be alarmed by the monster I had become.

"You remember me? Lena? I used to change your didies. I took you v'en you first vent valking. I taught you to say Svedish."

"Yes, yes," I said, pushing my recollections back as far as they would go. "Why, Lena! How nice of you to come."

"I read about you in the paper," she said. "I been very proud. I tell all my friends, 'She was my first baby.' "

"Lena," I said, when I could disengage myself, "this is my husband. I want you to meet my husband."

"Your husband?" cried Lena in astonishment. "Your *husband!* I t'ought he was yust—*a man!*"

Was there a shade of disappointment in her surprise? Had my glamour lost something of the ruddy glow of Hollywood? The person who had opened the door for her was only my husband—not a man. Her life must have been full of minor disappointments.

4

Mrs. Santa Claus

THE LADY WHO functioned as postmistress or assistant to the postmaster in our town in the year 1900 must have been a nice person. I don't know her name and I probably never saw her, but I have a letter from her that I prize.

I was not quite five years old in 1900, but I know how I looked. My mother and her friend across the street had their children photographed together. A little girl with tight blond curls and high-buttoned shoes, a little boy in a double-breasted suit, and both of us adorned with large campaign buttons depicting McKinley and Teddy Roosevelt. Our flagrant political partisanship certainly came from our parents, for we were more interested in small red wagons and wheelbarrows and dolls and dogs than in presidents and vice presidents. That year is pretty hazy to me, but by the next year I remember more and I have a clear political vignette of 1901.

I was sitting at a dressing table in my grandmother's house, and my mother or my aunt was brushing my hair. Suddenly someone rushed in and cried, "The president has been shot! McKinley has been shot by an anarchist." The horror of the grownups communicated itself to me. I had worn a McKinley button. In a sense he belonged to me. So I remember his assassination as I remember the poisoning of my dog.

But the year 1900 is very nearly blank for me. Yet I must have been carrying on a busy and imaginative life. I had a fictitious friend named Did. The name was convenient. When I felt guilty about something that I had done, I said, "Did did it," then I felt better.

Sometime during that summer I wrote a letter to Santa Claus. Someone must have helped me with it, for I'm sure that I could not write or spell. Who gave me the notion of Santa Claus in the middle of summer? And how did the letter come to be mailed? All of this is shrouded in the mists of time. Yet I must have asked for specific things and put the letter in the mailbox with high hopes.

In my mind's eye I see a kindly middle-aged lady with a black apron over a neat gray dress. She has had children of her own or else she has wished that she had. She is sorting the out-going mail and suddenly she is brought up short by an oddly scrawled and un-stamped envelope:

SANTA CLAUS

NORTH POLE

The sight of it must have lowered the summer temperature by several degrees. The kind-hearted postal clerk is puzzled. Should she open it or throw it in the waste basket? The light sparkles on her glasses as she looks at it. She puts up a hand and absently smooths back mouse-gray hair. For a moment she hesitates, wavering toward the waste basket. Then she makes up her mind and opens the untidy envelope. There is no record of what was written inside. Did she read the letter with laughter or pity or love for a casually known child?

At Christmas time that year I received a package addressed to me, not to any of the grown-ups, but to me. Inside the package was a small blue book called *Skyward and Back* by Lucy M. Robinson, copyright 1895. It did not provide very entertaining reading:

My Sphere

Look at my sphere.
It is round.
It can stand.
It can roll.
Roll, roll little sphere.
My sphere can spin.
Spin, spin little sphere.
Spin round and round.

The pictures were dull too, but I colored them, and sometimes I used the book to teach a row of stupidly staring dolls. So why have I kept the small blue book so long? Because on the flyleaf of the book, in a neat, intelligent handwriting is the following letter:

Dear Carol

You remember last summer you wrote to me and asked me for several things. I think you will get them all, but I send you this as a special reminder of me and I hope you will enjoy the story and be a good girl this coming year. I wish you a very Merry Christmas.

Mrs. Santa Claus

Christmas 1900

Mrs. Santa Claus! I shall never know her true name, but to me she is a very real person. The lady who functioned as postmistress or assistant to the postmaster in our town in the year 1900 must have been a nice person. I don't know her name and I probably never saw her, but I have a letter from her that I prize.

5

Johnny

IT IS DIFFICULT to know how much one may trust a child's judgment of character. When I was young, I formed instant likes and
dislikes; most of them, I am sure, were founded on personal whim
or emotion. Even as an adult, I could never look with kindness on
a certain successful businessman of our town because he had come
to the door, when I was a small child, to tell us that our dog had
been poisoned. He had nothing to do with the poisoning and he came
in neighborly kindness to give my mother the sad news. But, peer-
ing around her skirts, I saw him as a wicked man. I loved my dog,
so all through my life I distrusted and disliked the man who had
brought news of my dog's death.

Was it only because Johnny Guthrie was kind to me that I still
feel loyal to him? I have not heard his name for many years and I
do not know what finally became of him. Yet I still see him, young,
gay, a fine laughing figure of a boy who is immortal as long as my
memory serves me.

Later I heard the grown-ups talking about him, how he had rebelled against the polite social group into which he was born, how
he had taken things that did not belong to him, how he had disgraced
his family. I do not know the details of his crimes. Whether they
were kept from me on purpose because I was still a young child,
or whether I have put them aside as inconsequential, I do not know.
My memory is full of brilliant scenes, and long dark blanks.

I was five years old when my father died. He did not die at home
as most men did in those days. The doctors had sent him to Arizona
to try and recapture his health, and he got only as far as San Francisco
before he became too ill to go farther. One of his brothers was with
him there, and Uncle Henry wired to my mother and grandmother

and me to come if we were to see him alive. But we had a long journey and my father could not wait for us. By the time we reached San Francisco he was dead.

I was a delicate child and somehow, in all the turmoil of sorrow and cold trains and hasty meals, I arrived in San Francisco with a heavy chest cold and a high fever. My grandmother and uncle took my father's body home for burial, and my mother stayed on with me, lest she would lose the only other precious thing she had. It must have been a terrible time for her. I remember nothing of it, except that I gradually emerged from a long dark tunnel of illness into a half-light of convalescence.

It was nearly Christmas when I began to walk about again, but no one thought it safe to take me back into the snowy North until I was stronger. We lived in a small rented apartment, and I remember that one day I tried to make myself a piece of toast on a gas ring and burned my fingers. Such odd things a child remembers! The rest of our stay in that dark, bare apartment left no impression on my mind.

My father had been a representative of a Scottish life insurance company which had its main American office in San Francisco. The head of the company in the United States was a Scottish gentleman by the name of Guthrie. He and his wife must have pitied my mother in her difficult situation. There may even have been some slight feeling of culpability involved, for I learned later that Mr. Guthrie had been responsible for getting my father to audit the books of another young Scotsman in the company who had died of tuberculosis. The books were in very bad order and my father, in a winter when he was overworked and frail himself, had spent many evenings over them, trying to put them in order for the company.

At any rate the Guthries invited us to come and spend the Christmas holidays with them in their big house in the country. As I remember it, there were four teen-aged sons and a daughter in the household. The daughter like myself had been ill and was still in bed when we arrived. This was the era when young ladies coquetted behind fans, and I remember that my mother had brought her a beautiful little fan for a present.

From the dark, unremembered time of our stay in San Francisco, I now have a series of brightly colored and detailed pictures of our Christmas at the Guthries. In the first of these I see my mother and myself being ushered into the light and gracious room of the daughter of the house. I remember seeing her in bed with lace and prettiness about her, and of feeling proud that we had made her happy by giving her a fan.

This was in every part a lovely, gracious house, finer than anything I had seen before. I think that my mother may have been a little nervous in this opulent atmosphere at first, but she was pretty and looked well in her widow's weeds. She was an accomplished pianist, and her music soon put her at ease with people.

Although it was a lavishly furnished house, it was a house of rigorous morality, high and simple religious endeavor. The knowledge of this is strongly with me now and I am sure that I sensed it myself, for I do not recall having been told about it later. In our small northwestern town Victorianism was as superficial as the antimacassars and as easily removed, but here even I felt its roots going deeply and solidly through every phase of family life, even to family prayers which were attended by the servants. Charity was here, but it was cloaked with graciousness. The young people were all very kind to me, and, if my mother and I were the Guthries' Christian good deed for the season, we were happy and pleased to be there.

Only one of the four boys stands out for me. The other three are shadowy figures. Johnny was the next to the oldest, a tall, well-built boy with curly dark hair and red cheeks. He laughed and lifted me up to his shoulder where he liked to perch me. At first I was a little frightened, at the same time that I was delighted. To be carried high on a shoulder where I could see everything, this was a new and exciting experience.

"Be careful, Johnny," they said. I think that they had always said to Johnny, "Be careful," until he had almost ceased to hear it. But the kindness was stronger than the rebellion in him, and I trusted him.

On the night before Christmas the folding doors were closed to the library, but I knew that they had brought a very large evergreen tree in there and that they were trimming it. I was excited and curious. Life seemed to be gay to me once more, a thing to remember and enjoy. I sat with my mother in the parlor where she was reading a book, then I heard the sounds of smothered laughter and the scraping of a ladder on the floor and the tinkle of a bell.

The daughter was up again by now, and I heard her cry, "No, not there! Put it farther to the right." I was consumed with curiosity to see what they were doing.

Then Johnny came in from the garden where he had been on some errand of his own. He saw me sitting on the little stool by my mother, and he cried:

"What! Aren't they letting you help?"

"No," I said.

"Would you like to?"

"Yes."

"Come, then," he said. He swung me up onto his shoulder and pushed open the folding doors. The others were setting the unlighted candles in place. The tree was a huge and lovely thing covered with tinsel and colored balls.

"Oh!" I cried, "Oh!"

The other young people looked around at us then and shouted in consternation. Their faces were dark with disapproval.

"It was to be a surprise for her. Oh, now you have spoiled it for her! Johnny, how could you?"

"She is missing the best part," Johnny said. "You should have let her help."

"But no!" they cried. "It was to be a surprise. Take her away. She shouldn't see it until it is lighted."

I felt the four of them standing together against Johnny and me.

"Can't you see?" he said. "This is the part she would enjoy most. When it's all lighted, it will be over in a minute. This is the part she should share in."

I do not remember how it was resolved. I do not even remember the tree after it was lighted. It is only that moment which has endured for me, the moment of seeing the tree from Johnny's shoulder in all of its half-decked splendor and mystery, and feeling that he understood and knew what was best for me.

I have one more memory of that time, and it was again from Johnny's shoulder. Perhaps it was the afternoon of Christmas day, perhaps the day after. The sun shone brightly but the air was brisk and cool. Some of the young people set off now to walk to a small pond on the property where they amused themselves by sailing toy boats. I think that this was something they had done as children, and that they brought out the boats again for my amusement. I remember one boat in particular. It was perhaps three feet long and beautifully modeled of dark wood. The other boys went ahead of us, carrying the boats, and Johnny took me on his shoulder.

We went a long way by a path across a field where long brown marsh grass was knee high. The grass was bending in the brisk wind, and the sky was very blue. It seemed that I had never seen blue sky before, and the pond, when we came near it, was blue too.

Johnny laughed and talked to me and made jokes that a five-year-old child would understand. I remember the boats on the blue water, and the boys running around to the other side of the pond, bringing them to land, resetting their sails so that they would return again to the side where I stood holding Johnny's hand. I remember it all so clearly, yet nothing remarkable happened to fix it in my mind.

In the windy air, however, there was something which I did not understand, yet it was real to me. I have it still, the feeling that we were two sides of something: That there were the proper people, the right people; and that somehow Johnny was rebellious against them and was standing alone in opposition to them. Except for the little girl whom he had temporarily hoisted to his shoulder, he would have had no one on his side. For the moment in our loneliness, in our uniqueness, we were as one against the others.

Do children really grasp the essence of character? I do not know. I only hope it was as happy a day for Johnny Guthrie as it was for me.

6

Mama

M Y MOTHER WANTED something from life that she did not find. I have thought about her very often throughout my life, and my knowledge of her has grown through my own experience. Yet the more light that surrounds her, the more mysterious she becomes. She is illumined but not clarified or explained, and my own attitude toward her has changed as I have changed.

I was eight years old when she died by her own hand – a very beautiful woman, so people tell me, and a gifted musician. By the age of eight a child should have amassed a great many memories. Yet the little jewel-clear visions that I have of my mother are few and seem to lead toward nothing. After her death I greatly revered her memory, and (now I think largely through the efforts of my aunt) I thought of her as something lovely and lost, unattainable and precious. "Mama," my lost one. They kept from me very carefully the fact that she had taken her own life, but I believe that intuitively I always knew, for when at eighteen or nineteen I was told the truth, it was neither a shock nor a surprise, but only a rude bringing into the open of what had been tacitly understood.

What I remember of her is woven and intertwined with what they have told me, as the solid and upright trees of the jungle are woven and intertwined with the fantastic vines. So that I seem to hear her voice saying, as she looked on my infant face, "Well, you're not very pretty, but your mother loves you anyway." But did she really love me? The older I grow, the less I think so.

One reason I think so is the persistent memory I have of another woman, a woman whose name I do not even know. This memory has been warm and strong with me throughout my life. It is completely detached and alone, a little wedge-shaped picture which does not fit into the jigsaw puzzle yet is always there on the board. It keeps coming to hand. "Here. Here. I belong in here." But color and outline are incongruous. Why have I kept it then? Because it was strange and precious perhaps, something unexpected and too comforting to let go.

I am in bed for the night in a semi-darkened room which is strange to me, and a strange woman comes and lies beside me to make me feel less strange. Gradually I have surrounded this detached picture with meager facts. For some reason I had been taken with my mother and her second husband on a trip to a neighboring town. I was usually left at home because my aunt and grandmother lived next door, and were glad to look after me. I must have been about seven years old, a very blonde, pale child, silent and not very rugged physically. There was a ball or party of some kind in the strange town, and we stayed with an elderly colonel who was an important man and had a big house and a young wife but no children.

I was put to bed in a large double bed in a room alone while my mother and her husband went to the party. I do not remember their departure. I had no feeling of separation nor resentment. Only the room was strange and I was alone. But I had learned to accept with the stoicism of the silent, unloved child. What I remember so clearly now is that the door opened with a breaking and closing of light, and that the colonel's young wife came and lay beside me on top of the double bed. She talked to me very sweetly and gently so that I should not feel strange in a house that was unfamiliar. What did she tell me? I can't remember. Perhaps it was a story, something simple and old and suited to the ears of a child. But a great warmth flowed from her to me, a tenderness I had wanted but not had. And perhaps I satisfied in her some unfulfilled maternity.

I am not sure how much I have deepened the colors of this bit by going over them, but it seems to me that she had fluffy dark hair and that she wore some kind of lacy-silky negligee or wrapper and that she had a smell of flowers. If I have sentimentalized this picture, it is as significant as that I should remember it at all.

Enveloped in security and love and trust, I went to sleep. In my memory the next day never dawns. I do not know how we returned to our town, nor what we had for breakfast, nor what the lady said to me later, nor how she looked in morning light. This is an isolated piece. Yet, after many years, I think that I can fit it in. Even though my mother must have fondled me and taken me upon her lap or held me in her arms or even lain beside me on a bed a great many times in the eight years we were together, I cannot remember one of them. There must have been in her embrace something perfunctory and unfelt; a duty done toward a little, homely child who did not occupy the center of her heart. And, while I did not understand what it was she failed to give me, I recognized it in the other woman. So for many years I have kept this odd piece warm and vivid with the gratitude of a lonely child, and somewhere it fits here in the puzzle.

7

My Dearest Friends

DOGS WERE MY love and my delight. They helped to make a lonely childhood bearable. We had all kinds, not a distinguished breed among them, and their characters were as diversified as their antecedents. The first great tragedy of my life was connected with the poisoning of my first dog. Some fanatic in town was always poisoning dogs. So far as I know he was never caught, but how many children grieved because of him. Few losses in my life have seemed greater to me than this loss. I could not have been more than three or four years old and I remember it very clearly. After that there were other dogs, all greatly beloved, my dearest friends!

Once, when I was probably six years old and unhappy both at home and at the school which I had just begun to attend, there was a horrible afternoon when some older child told me that my dog had been poisoned. It was a cold, raw day with sleet in the air and slush underfoot. I rushed home with wildly beating heart, trying to blink back tears. It had been announced to me before that my dog had been poisoned, and it had been so. I had seen his stiff, bloated body lying on the lawn. So now it must be true that it had happened again, and this time I really could not bear it. I was frightened of school, it seemed strange and awful, and there was a strange and angry man in our house instead of my gentle father. I ran home through the chilly wet, my head bare, my feet soaking, and the house was empty. My mother had gone out somewhere. My dog was not there.

I remember how I ran all about the neighborhood, calling and crying, calling and crying. No one came to help me, and I had not yet formed the habit of going to my grandmother.

At last I went home again, shivering with cold but no longer crying. When terrible things happen, one had to accept them; crying did no good. When I went in, my mother was there getting supper. The man had not come home. The warm blaze glowed behind the isinglass panes in the base burner, and lying on the rug before the fire was my dog. My dog! He had not been poisoned after all. He got up and stretched and wagged his tail.

"You're very late coming home from school," my mother said. "However did you get so wet?" But all I could do was hold my dog and let him lick my face.

I remember the many dogs, so gay and loyal and dependable when humans failed. I remember the pleasant smell of little puppies, all the same, "like turnips" Aunt used to say, and how their skins were loose and slippery, and their feet big and awkward.

Gram was expert at training dogs to become good citizens. She used to say that a dog reflected the character of his master, and if you found an ill-tempered and badly behaved dog, you could look for the trouble in the man who owned him. She used to crop the puppies' tails herself, and sometimes she spayed cats. I never could bear to watch the cropping of the puppies' tails, but she said it didn't hurt them if they were quite young and you were careful to cut between the tail bones with a sharp knife. "Only a drop of blood," she said, "and the puppy doesn't even yelp. He'll make a finer looking dog when he is grown."

I owe so much to animals of many kinds, horses, cats, even chickens, but especially to dogs. And how can one say thank you to them? I keep a membership in the Humane Society, only because it is one of the few ways in which I can make some return for what they have done for me.

8

Gram

M Y RELATIONSHIP TO my grandmother was a very special one. She represented for me stability, security, wisdom and good sense. These things had been lacking in much of my earliest life, and I prized them when I found them. In a sense she also represented romance, for her vivid stories of her own childhood on a pioneer frontier gave me my first feeling of continuity with the past, a past more exciting and strange than my own. I expect that I have glamorized her unduly. She was a quiet old woman who had allowed herself to get too fat. She seldom left her house to go anywhere—certainly not socially. Her interests were not broad, her opinions not unusual. Ostensibly a heart condition kept her at home, but a more restless person would have gone out in spite of an uncertain heart. She had infinite calm and self-content, and the world outside had in many ways treated her so cruelly that she did well to shun it. She made her own world at home, and, if anyone wished to find her there, she was good-tempered and available. People had to come to her.

Gram enjoyed men's chores and was never happier than mending a fence, knocking together a chicken coop, repairing a clock or a doorlock, or spading up a garden plot. But she was competent indoors too, baking bread and large, thick cookies sprinkled with caraway seed.

I can see her hands yet, wrinkled, roughened, marked with brown age spots, as she handled the jackknife with which she had just cut a succulent section of box elder twig to make me a whistle. With the handle of the knife she tapped the tender bark of the twig, turning the twig in her fingers to bruise the bark evenly. Then with care she slipped the green bark from the slippery white wood and set it aside while she made a slender cut in the wood, being careful not to reach the center pith. Lastly she cut a notch in the sheaf of bark and slipped it back over the wood. It had become a neat green whistle, and I was the first to blow it and to try its individual note.

She loved a keenly sharpened knife and she used to carve cherry pits into tiny baskets for my doll's delight. She made tops for me out of empty spools by fitting them with a wooden core that served both as handle and sharply whittled spinning point. I used to try to imitate her skill with a jackknife, and I remember one occasion when I cut my finger and went indoors for a bandage. In a few moments I went out again and continued cutting the half-rotted wood that I had selected for its ease in carving. I see the brown pithy wood still, although I have forgotten what I was trying to carve. I cut myself again and went indoors for another bandage. But I was stubborn and I returned to my carving. When I had cut myself for the third time, Gram said, "Come, Kit. That's enough. My knife is too sharp for you."

Gram never engaged in the kind of ornamental "fancywork" that her sister Hetty and her daughter loved to do. The nearest she came to it was the time she made me a necklace by stringing blue and yellow beads into a circlet of forget-me-nots. What interested her was not making a forget-me-not necklace but the ingenuity it required to string the blue and yellow beads in such a way that the yellow center was surrounded by six tiny blue petals—more of a job for an engineer than for a lady doing fancywork.

But most of her handiwork was of an extremely utilitarian nature. She had a friend who worked in a tailor's shop, and, when the tailor's sample books were out of date, the friend used to bring Gram the rectangular swatches of heavy woolen materials to make into quilts. Gram ran these swatches together on the sewing machine—a brown square here, a gray square there, a black with thin white stripes next—a very drab-looking set of patches. A thin layer of cotton went inside the quilt and it was backed with gray outing flannel and tied at the corner of each woolen square with a small tack of red yarn. I have such a quilt, heavy and warm and guaranteed to outlast several generations of perishable people. It is ugly and thrifty, and somehow it contains the very essence of Gram's integrity.

I remember her long, wavy, beautiful hair which had been auburn when she was young. When she brushed it out, it hung long and thick below her waist so that she could sit on the ends. It was liberally streaked with gray as I knew her, but never quite white even at age eighty-six. She used to coil it up in a thick bun on the top of her head, and two little curls escaped on either side of her forehead. It was the lively and abundant kind of hair that I associate with great physical vitality. She used to tell how the girls made the "spit curls" that were fashionable when she was young. They made a gelatinous liquid from quince seeds and plastered the formal curls flat on their temples or cheeks. They also pierced their ears for earrings by running a hot needle through the lobe and then sticking a broom straw through the hole to keep it open until the healing was complete.

Gram had large ears which I have inherited. She used to say that large ears were a sign of generosity, and in fact she set great store on discerning character by the appearance of physical features. She was proud of her high-bridged nose which she fondly called "Roman." She had a paper-covered book on phrenology which showed a human cranium divided into various sectors and zones of influence.

When a young man came calling on me in my university days, Aunt did all the talking until we could make our escape to a concert or the movies. Gram said never a word, but her sharp hazel eyes took in everything about the new young man. The next morning I would have a complete character analysis from Gram.

"Kit, he wouldn't make a good husband." (A good husband was the farthest thing from my mind at that stage of my life, and I bore her summings up with the patience of a martyr.) "His forehead is too narrow, his eyes too closely set. He'll think more of himself than he will of his wife. Look at his chin, too, no strength of will, and his mouth is loose."

"Why, Mama," Aunt would say, "I thought he was very good looking, quite distinguished, and *such* a good conversationalist." She meant a listener, of course.

"He's all right for a good time," Grandma said. "Just don't get too serious, my child." Her character analyses were not all unfavorable.

Some of the dullest boys, in my opinion, would make the best husbands, according to Gram and the phrenologists.

Aunt loved new young men at first sight. But after they had called on me more than three times she began to pick flaws with them; after five or six calls, she refused to speak to them.

Like Job, my grandmother was plagued with many tribulations. She was persuaded out of marrying the man she really loved because he drank and her parents were convinced that she could not reform him. She bore eight children and lost five in infancy; of the three who survived, only one was a comfort to her—and sometimes a trial as well. Her husband was murdered just after he had let his insurance policy lapse, so that she inherited a little property and a lot of unpaid bills. She reared one grandchild and partly reared two others. She worked hard and managed her life with dignity and good humor. What did she get out of it? A step-by-step and day-by-day satisfaction of daylight and dark, of turning seasons, of gardens and flowers and friendly animals, of sharp knives and clocks that were on time, of well-baked bread and a properly stuffed and roasted chicken, of rich memories of a happy childhood. She took great store in her happy childhood, and perhaps I, who have had so much more happy and fortunate a life than she had, have inherited her tendency to look backwards to my beginnings with appreciation and understanding. Why else am I writing this?

My cousin Tom,[7] who lived with Gram after my Aunt and I had both left, says, "If there is any good in me, I owe it to Gram." It is a broad statement, but I think that I can say the same. She never preached or scolded. She was never possessive or overbearing, but it was impossible to live with her and not be infected with some of her honor and justice and good humor.

I remember a time when I was clowning around the kitchen while I was wiping dishes for her. I balanced a pile of plates on one hand while I pranced to the cupboard to put them away.

"Take care, Kit. You'll have an accident," she said. A few moments later I did. A pile of plates went crashing down and smashed all over the floor. Knowing that I deserved it, I honestly expected a terrible punishment.

"Well," said Gram in a mild voice, "accidents *will* happen in the best regulated families." She loved aphorisms and cliches, and knew *Poor Richard's Almanac* better than the Bible. "Keep thy shop and thy shop will keep thee." "A penny saved is a penny earned." "Teach your head to save your heels." She had a saying for every occasion.

But she was capable of righteous anger, too. Tom tells how proud he felt because at the end of the month she would entrust him with the hard-come-by money to pay the grocer's and the butcher's bills. He was about eight years old, and, when he had paid the grocer's bill, the grocer was in the habit of giving him a little striped bag of hard candies as a bonus for prompt payment. One day the grocer forgot, and Tom went home empty-handed and on the verge of tears. Gram was affronted. No matter how hard it was to find the money, she always paid her bills on time. She went to the telephone and rang the grocery store.

"How does it happen that you did not give my grandson a bag of candy when he paid the bill?" There was thunder and lightning in her voice.

"Well, Mrs. Watkins, it must have been an oversight."

"He'll be right down to get it," Grandma said, "and don't forget next time."

Gram was famous for her mincemeat. Once the members of the ladies aid society of the church asked if they could bring the ingredients to her house and have her help them make the mincemeat for a church supper. They mixed the chopped apples and raisins and suet and spices and cider according to the recipe, and they kept tasting and tasting.

"But, Mrs. Watkins, it doesn't taste like your mincemeat. Perhaps we are making too large a quantity. It doesn't have the proper flavor."

"Just a minute," Gram said. She went behind a closet door where she kept a cherished brandy bottle, and emptied half of its contents into the mincemeat. This was a part of her secret that she never disclosed to the Presbyterians. When the mixture was well stirred, she asked the ladies to taste again.

"Oh, *what* did you do to it?" they cried. "Now it has the proper flavor. It's simply delicious." She didn't tell the ladies what had made the difference. It might have bothered their consciences.

My grandmother has crept into nearly every book that I have written. Sometimes she is the chief character, sometimes she has a minor part; sometimes she is young, sometimes she is old. Then again it is only her spirit that shapes the writing, together with the things she taught me. Her own writing was laborious. She was left-handed, and they had made her use her right hand in the penmanship classes at school. She might have become a stutterer, but apparently her rugged character had brought her through the rigors of right-hand training with no ill effects. Only her handwriting was always odd and difficult to read.

But she was a matchless storyteller who could select the dramatic essentials from humdrum material and make us laugh and sigh over things that had happened long ago. Aunt was a good storyteller too, but she was likely to add fictitious details and embellishments to such an extent that I never dared repeat her stories for fear that someone might call me a liar. But Gram knew how to make a very good story out of nothing but true facts. Years later, when I wrote down the stories she had so often told me, I discovered to my astonishment that I had written history.

A childhood case of scarlet fever had left Gram deaf in one ear. If you happened to be on the wrong side of her you had to shout. But she accepted this as philosophically as she accepted the other tragedies of her life. "It's very easy to go to sleep," she said. "I just turn my good ear to the pillow and everything is quiet."

Perhaps the thing I learned from her that has been most valuable to me is acceptance. My aunt never learned happy acceptance. When it was thrust upon her as a final necessity, she still rebelled.

After working all day around the house and in the yard and reading the daily newspaper, Gram liked to sit down in the old platform rocker beside the baseburner in the dining room, fold her hands across her stomach and rock very gently back and forth. If she closed her eyes, it was not to sleep. Aunt, who could not bear to see inaction of any kind, used to cry in exasperation, "Mama, how can you endure *sitting* there, without *doing* anything?"

"Well, dear," Gram replied mildly, "I was thinking."

9

Aunt Elsie

WHEN I WENT to live with my grandmother, my aunt Elsie took me over with a devotion and deep sincerity of affection that completely engulfed me. At last I was beloved. I was so grateful that I might have been utterly possessed had not adversity planted a little core of resistance in me which stood me in good stead. No matter how much my aunt loved me and accepted me as her life work and *raison d'etre,* I nourished a small seed of individuality that kept me from being completely her thing.

My aunt and I shared a bedroom upstairs in an old house that was essentially one-story. A dark enclosed stairway with a turn in it led up from the kitchen to a large, airy bedroom under the eaves in the old part of the house. It had a double window looking out toward the poplar-lined street and the Presbyterian Church, and a side window that overlooked the side yard and the house which my mother had built and which was now occupied by a family of friends. At the top of the narrow twisting stairway was a little hall, quite dark when the bedroom door was closed, and here were bookshelves where the overflow books from the parlor were stored – complete sets of Bulwer-Lytton, Charles Read, and other half-forgotten Victorian novelists. In the bedroom I had another shelf with books of my own.

Although she slept with me in the same bed, my aunt in her generosity had dedicated the room to me. It contained the light curley-maple dressing table, rocker, dressing table, chair, and chest of drawers that had been in my room at my mother's house, and the three-quarter brass bed. There was a wash stand by the window with a large bowl and water pitcher decorated with blue roses. The pictures had come out of my room at the other house. My aunt wanted me to feel at home here, I am sure, and I did, although I did not need the things from the unhomelike house next door to make me feel so.

Now, as I think back, where were my aunt's things? It is true that her comb and brush and hair receiver, her cosmetics and her pincushion were on my dressing table, and her clothes hung along with mine in the long, dark closet. But she had dedicated herself so completely to me that I seem to remember nothing else in the room belonging to her.

Three steps up from the bedroom was a huge unfinished attic over the parlor. It may once have been intended to be finished into bedrooms, before the lives of the various babies of my grandparents flickered out. Now it contained trunks full of memories and all sorts of flotsam and jetsam of family life. On rainy days it was a source of interest and pleasure to me when other forms of entertainment palled.

By the steps to the attic I had a wonderful doll house — wonderful to me because I had made it myself out of two orange crates set on end and fastened together with a peaked roof that naturally provided the dolls with an attic. I had papered and painted and furnished the house with doll furniture I had made out of spools and boxes or had saved my allowance to purchase from the toy store. Two small, fat dolls named Elsie and Eileen lived in the doll house. I had many other dolls of all sizes and shapes and I never played "baby" with them, but I put them through long, complicated plays and life stories that sometimes took days and weeks to enact. I expect that Aunt was the one who picked them up when they were strewn across the floor.

The bedroom was heated in winter by a register or small double grating of ironwork let into the floor over the baseburner in the dining room below. The papered-over brick chimney that went up the wall behind the register also conducted some cheerful heat. In the cold snowy mornings of winter, Aunt rose with missionary goodness and went downstairs to start fires in the baseburner and the big kitchen range. From my cozy bed I would sometimes hear her chopping kindling, although the fire in the kitchen range was usually allowed to go out early enough the previous evening so that a new fire could be laid in readiness for the morning match.

There was a tin matchbox tacked up in the kitchen beside the door to the dining room. Sometimes Aunt and I and assorted young friends used to have kicking competitions to see who could kick high enough to knock the matches out of the box.

Particularly on school mornings I lay snugly abed, dreading the moment when I must get up. But finally Aunt would call, "Up, up, Mary, and see the sun rise." This was a quotation from the old joke about the child who had been taught to say "double t" in spelling "letter," and so, when confronted by the exhortation to Mary in his reading book, read, "Double up, Mary, and see the sun rise."

I would then reluctantly arise, break the thin crust of ice on the water pitcher to wash my face, and, in a luxury of warmth, I would stand over the heat register to dress. I wore a long, full outing flannel nightgown, and the hot air, rising from the dining room below, would blow my nightgown like a white balloon about my skinny legs. After I had struggled to get my long winter underwear that went *down* tucked into my long black stockings that went *up,* my legs no longer looked skinny. Presently I was ready for breakfast.

My aunt was one of the most self-sacrificing persons in the world. She would never let anyone do anything for her, and so we were often forced into the guilty feeling that we were hopelessly in her debt. She suffered unselfishly in our behalf. Yet it gave her a hold over us that was sometimes frightening. Out of her excessive goodness and generosity she wrought bands of iron.

When I was small, she shared most of my thoughts and interests. She led my friends and me on walks and picnics. In the early spring she was the one who led us out the railroad tracks (the roads were too muddy) to find the first pussywillows; in the summer she made the sandwiches and deviled eggs and packed them in the pony cart for our consumption beside some small stream where we could wade. If I forgot to feed my pets, she did it for me. If I went into the kitchen to make messy cookies or candy, she said, "Here, darling, let me do it for you. Aunty can do it so much more quickly." At night I went to sleep with her protective arm around me. When I finally rebelled against this she moved to one of the back bedrooms downstairs and

I was gloriously alone in the room over the baseburner. But I knew that she was hurt. It was the same with my thoughts; when they began to be private and my own, she never forgave me for ceasing to share them aloud with her.

   She was the solace and the burden of my childhood.

10

Aunt Win

I HAVE SPENT MOST of my life disliking my Aunt Win. I disliked her because she ran away from an amiable husband and two little boys that I loved, and because she came to my poor and thrifty grandmother for financial help whenever she had squandered her latest windfalls. I disliked her because, in the midst of our harmonious tranquility, she would arrive like a whirlwind, set us all akimbo, and leave everyone in tears, bruised and wounded for days, while she went away happily relieved of her tension. Perhaps I disliked her because she was only a few years older than I and never toadied to me as my aunt Elsie did.

But I have gradually come to think of her dispassionately as an interesting person and to bury old animosities in an attempt at understanding. She was a kind of natural genius. She could play any melody that she heard on the piano without ever knowing a note of music, and if she had been willing to discipline herself she could probably have become a first-class concert pianist. As it was, she made up in runs and trills what she lacked in precision and finesse.

My mother was an excellent musician, but she was willing to study and practice to become proficient. Aunt Win was under the curse of never having to try. Nature had handed her a wonderful gift and she was too lazy or careless or unambitious to perfect it. Yet the talent nagged at her and she liked applause. In late life she made some study of the organ, and she played for a long time on a radio station and gave music lessons. Her real pleasure, however, lay in the wandering life of the evangelists. I don't think that her religion ever went very deep, but she loved the gypsy atmosphere of the evangelistic tents and she played with "soul," with emotional embellishments and many runs and flourishes. The old hymns hummed and crackled under her nimble fingers, and the preachers could not have lured so many people to the mourner's bench without her background of weeping or rejoicing music.

My aunt Win was born a couple of generations before her time. In 1910 nobody understood her. In 1970 she would have been the belle of Carnaby Street. She wore her red hair in a perfect Afro hairdo. Marriage to her was a prelude to divorce (between lesser trial encounters with the opposite sex), and she would have made a marvelous extemporizing member of the Memphis Maulers, the Hot Potatoes, or the Tin Pan Troubadours. She made her own rules and regulations, or rather she discarded all those made by other people, and she would have adored credit cards.

When her father, the doctor, was suddenly removed from her life by an assassin's bullet, she was a little red-haired girl of twelve. She was his baby and he had adored her. He took her riding with him in his buggy on country calls. He bought her dresses that he had never afforded for the other girls. He showed her off with pride to all his friends. When he and Gram entertained guests, it was little red-haired Winnie and the dog Mac who did the entertaining. After dinner when the guests assembled in the parlor, Winnie came in and sat down at the piano and Mac began to roll over and walk on his hind legs without being told to do so.

"Doctor, you are spoiling both of them," Gram said. "You shouldn't allow them to occupy the center of the stage before company. It isn't good for their characters."

"Characters!" jeered Grandfather. "Who's talking about characters? They're cute, they're smart. Let them show off as much as they like." And Winnie, who had stood by listening, looked at her mother triumphantly and said, "You see what Papa says!"

"Didn't you hear them all laughing and applauding?" Grandpa said. "There isn't another kid in town, her age or any age, can play piano like my baby. And as to Mac, well, he's a smart dog and he knows it."

Mac was a black dog with tight black curls, a bastard poodle. He continued performing gratuitously until old age defeated him.

But Winnie was left bereft when Grandfather died. He had laughed at her tantrums. "What can you expect of a feisty little redhead?" he said indulgently.

"Doctor, you just encourage her in all her naughtiness."

"Why should you complain, Cad? The red hair comes from your side of the family."

"But we were taught to govern our tempers for the sake of other people, not to indulge them for the sake of ourselves."

"Well, so she gets her tempers from me, eh? But she's a little genius, and that's on my side of the family, too, I guess."

Suddenly, with the loss of her chief applauder, Aunt Winnie at twelve found herself merely the youngest of three sisters, no longer Papa's ungoverned baby.

Now there was no more money for extravagant dresses; there were no more dinner parties with applauding guests in the parlor. No one took her to town and said to a ring of laughing men, "This is my daughter, Winifred. She's the genius and the beauty of the family."

Instead Grandma began with patience to try to undo some of the errors that had been made.

"Winnie, you must pick up your room and put your clothes in the closet. Elsie always does."

"Oh, Elsie, that stuffy old monument of virtue! Papa wouldn't have made me."

"I am *not* a stuffy old monument of virtue," Aunt Elsie would retort. "And I'm grieving for Papa too."

"*You* grieve! That makes me laugh. He loved me better than all of you. I'm the only one who feels how awful it is without him. I am the only one who cares."

It ended with anger and tears and sometimes shrieks of despair.

I was not an integral part of their life at this time, yet I witnessed many painful scenes of rebellion and frustration. I knew when Aunt Win had her moments of triumph: when she recited selections from *Enoch Arden* in school; when she wore a white cheesecloth Grecian robe to appear in a pageant; when she decided that she would become an actress; and when she discovered the opposite sex and began to go out with boys.

At sixteen she ran away from home and married a man who was twice her age. Was she trying to find Papa? Nobody knows. But if she was, she had chosen the wrong man. Her husband was a nice and gentle fellow, full of easy laughter, who had been a bachelor for a long time and who lived a mild and unexciting existence as teller in a local bank. Into his uneventful life she brought all the turbulence and discontent that she had removed from Grandma's house. But she continued to live close enough to Grandma's so that about once a week or perhaps once in two weeks she could bring a tantrum back with her. If not a full-sized hurricane, at least a noisy quarrel with her sister Elsie. She had an admiration for my mother's musical skill and beauty that kept her manners charming at our house. But something about her sister Elsie's ostentatious virtue made her explode into instant violence.

Among Aunt Winnie's many natural gifts was one for interior decorating. She was before her time in that too. No one had heard of "interior decoration" in that day. You rented an empty house; you ordered a dining room set, a bed and a chamber pot from the furniture dealer who was also the undertaker; and you set up housekeeping. Maybe you went so far as to hang a picture of Pharaoh's horses or an enlarged photograph of a deceased relative over the settee in the parlor, or maybe you put a bearskin rug on the floor in front of the baseburner, and that was it.

But my aunt Win satisfied her restless yearnings by taking a hopeless old house and filling it with bright curtains, imaginative furniture, pretty pictures, and a sense of grace and unity. She worked like a slave until she had achieved her effect. She painted and papered and cut and sewed. When the old house was completely rehabilitated and had become the admiration of her family and friends, she suddenly grew sick and tired of it. She sold it, sometimes at a loss to be rid of it in a hurry, but more often at a nice profit. But the money never went into her husband's bank; it was something to be deliciously squandered on the next project. She always owed more than she made. So she went through a series of hopeless old houses, making them not only habitable but beautiful, and she produced two very nice little boys. Then the era began to catch up with her, and someone invented the moving picture.

I can still hear her improvising on the old piano in the pit of the Unique Theater. ("Uni*cue*," we children called it.) Below the screen on which the silent black and white movies flickered and danced, my aunt sat enthroned, queen of the flicks, manipulator of the heart throbs of the town. I might sometimes be holding hands in the balcony with a shy admirer, but still I was emotionally aware of Aunt Win playing her heart out as the film unrolled. Other people may claim the honor, but I am sure that it must have been Aunt Win who first played *William Tell* for the galloping sequences and who wrung tears from the hardiest with *Hearts and Flowers* during the sentimental passages. She played other things, too, gloriously and with abandon. Sometimes tears streamed down her face as she played, and, no matter how many times she gazed at the moving scenes above her, she could always put passion into the energy of her flying fingers.

But even the movies finally grew tiresome to her and she ran away with a good looking but notoriously unstable doctor who was quite a lot older than she was. Papa again? Perhaps. He was not from our town and he roamed the country – selling patent medicines? I'm not sure what. But it put her in motion, and that was what her soul craved.

Grandma and the virtuous Elsie and later a second wife who was responsible and kind took over the upbringing of the two little boys that Winnie had abandoned.

About this time she changed her name to "Wanda" and we heard of her less and less. Occasionally there were letters, written in a nice flowing hand and terribly spelled. Sometimes they were full of extravagant affection and sometimes of stormy abuse, but they nearly always ended on the same note: a plea for money.

"Mama darling – lend me a little money just to tyde me over a bad time – Ill pay you back as soon as I can.
>   With oshuns of love,
>   Wanda."

So Grandma scraped together some of her egg money and took some hoarded dollar bills from between the plates in the china cabinet or even went into the "strong box" that she hid in the lower part of the grandfather clock to befuddle burglars, and sent Wanda what she could. She did not expect to get it back. I think that Grandma had a kind of guilty feeling about Wanda. Because of Doctor's indulgences, the child had not been brought up properly; and the red hair did come from her side of the family—yet the Woodhouses, with all their red hair, had been responsible people, and not given to temper tantrums.

"Mama, you know you oughtn't to send her money," Aunt Elsie said. "You have so little and she makes plenty but she squanders it as fast as she gets her hands on it. You know you'll never see it again and she'll just ask for more. *I* never ask you for anything, Mama, do I?"

"No, dear, you never do. You are my dear, dependable daughter. But still Winnie is my baby. I can't let her go hungry."

Wanda soon broke up with her wandering doctor. She played in theaters in various rural towns. Later the radio caught up with her, and she played the organ over the air to ever-increasing numbers of listeners. But her great fulfillment came with the traveling evangelists. The time-worn hymns dripped off her fingers like honey off hotcakes. She syncopated them and embellished them with runs and tremolos; wild horses galloped in them; the cavalry arrived in the nick of time; and the sinners wept on Jesus' bosom. What the preachers could not accomplish with their oratory, Wanda could effect in a moment with her fingers on the keys. Her wanderlust, her need for applause, all her emotional hunger for sensation were fed and nourished in the gypsy tents of the evangelists.

There were always men who admired her and satisfied her vanity. But there came a time when even the vicissitudes of evangelism must have palled. She settled down in a smallish Oregon town and married a carpenter. I don't know how many houses she decorated for him, but presumably he could always build a new one. This was the most stable period of her life. She had an organ hour on the radio and she gave music lessons.

When Aunt Elsie and I were both married, Gram went to live with Wanda and Ted for a while. She approved of Ted and seemed to have had a happy time with them. Wanda could be very pleasant company when everything was going her way. But Gram decided that, after all, she had better go back to Elsie. My twelve-year-old daughter and I, for reasons of health, had spent a winter in Arizona, and it was arranged that, since we would be going back by a train which would pass through Wanda's town, we would pick up Gram at the station to take her on to Aunt Elsie's.

Aunt Wanda was at the station with Gram in a wheelchair. She was wearing a baseball cap because it shaded her eyes much better than a hat, and she never cared what other people thought about her clothing. But Wanda was the one first seen as the train drew into the station. Her kinky red hair stood out like an exaggerated halo all over her head. I had not seen her for years and would never see her again, but she was unmistakable.

We embraced all around and with the porter's help got Gram onto the train before the conductor cried, "All aboard."

"How was it, Gram?" I asked.

"Well, I had a nice time," Gram said. "Ted is a good man. I think he's the only one who could live with her for any length of time and get along. I'll be glad to get back again to Elsie."

A few years after this Ted died. We were all very sorry because, although none of us but Gram had ever seen him, we respected his character.

"And now she will be well fixed," Gram said. "Ted has been very thrifty, and she'll be left with enough to support her for the rest of her life if she is careful."

"Careful?" cried Aunt. "Whoever heard of Wanda being careful?"

"Perhaps she's learned," Grandma said, but there was no conviction in her voice.

So Wanda took Ted's life savings, and (because he had been such a good, patient husband and she owed him so much) she built him a large ornamental mausoleum. It overshadowed every puny monument in the cemetery, and it cost—yes, it did, all of Ted's life savings.

"Dear Mama—The mossoleum was much more expensive than the original estimate. I wonder, dear, if you could lend me a little bit to tyde me over. . . ."

She went back on the evangelistic circuit, and down, and down. When she died, she was living with a young Indian in an abandoned house and there was no food in the cupboard. She had lost track of all of us for a long time.

11

Old Fatty

OLD MAN RUMPSCHNICKEL was the meanest man that I knew in my childhood. He was also the only self-avowed atheist in a small western town that reverberated with the sound of many church bells on a Sabbath morning.

The Rumpschnickels lived around the corner from my grandmother's house, so that, although we faced on different streets, our backyards touched at one point. From Grandma's side windows we could see old man Rumpschnickel going downtown in the morning, stumping along in stubborn pride with his ample belly stuck out before him and a forbidding look on his face. At a distance, seeing his rotund figure, one might easily mistake him for the sort of man who would have a smile on his face and be followed by small children and dogs. But this was not the case.

He did not have an office downtown, in spite of the regular hours he kept, but he used to sit on a ledge in front of the pool hall with one or two other leisured gentlemen and watch the flow of business on our main street. He went downtown every day of the week and Sunday too, for it was a seven-day pool hall. He always went on the stroke of ten; by two o'clock he had had enough and he came home. Mrs. Rumpschnickel put dinner on then and this economized on food, for they needed only a light tea in the evening.

"There goes Old Pappy Rumpschnickel," my grandmother used to say when she saw him stumping down the hill, or "There goes Old Fatty Rumpschnickel." I never heard the man's first name, but, when Grandma called him Old Pappy or Old Fatty, it meant that she disapproved of him. Actually, I suppose, he was younger than she was, but she always prefixed the Pappy or Fatty with an Old. She did not disapprove of him so much because he was an atheist, for my grandmother was extremely tolerant with respect to belief. She thought that every person had a right to their own views, and she kept her own to herself, so that I do not know to this day exactly what hers were. But she strongly disapproved of meanness and injustice and she felt that Old Man Rumpschnickel was mean and unjust to his wife and his daughter.

The Rumpschnickels had retired from a large farm and come to spend their remaining years in town, living on the income of their early industry. Everybody knew everybody's business in our town, and, since the bankers were as fond of gossip as the rest of us, we had it on authority that Old Man Rumpschnickel was very rich. The house that he bought was a respectable one but it was furnished with great economy, and, if his wife wanted to put an extra egg in a cake when her limited monthly allowance at the grocery store was used up, she had to come and borrow the egg from my grandmother. (Gram had a chicken run in the backyard, and in those days, if we had nothing else, there were always eggs during the week and a stewing chicken for Sunday.)

Gram saw at once that Mrs. Rumpschnickel needed a friend, and Mrs. Rumpschnickel often came and sat in our kitchen to unburden herself over a cup of tea. She was a little, cross-eyed woman, very plain and shy, the perfect victim for a bullying husband. But they had a pretty and spirited daughter, named Eva, and it was ostensibly for Eva's education that they had moved to town.

Old Man Rumpschnickel proposed to give Eva a high school education, but, although she was a bright student and there was a college in town which she could have attended cheaply, he wanted no folderol of higher education. When she should finish high school, it was understood that she would go to work and repay her father all that he had expended on her.

The Rumpschnickels knew no one in town when they came, and, while the Old Man got his society in front of the pool hall, the missus had only my grandmother. She yearned for something more, and she had a great and overpowering longing for the consolations of religion.

"But he'll never let me join a church," she told my grandmother. "He curses perfectly awful if I ever mention churching. It would be a blow to his pride as an atheist."

My grandmother believed in women's rights. "Go ahead," she said. "Join a church if you want it. He won't kill you."

"I don't know," Mrs. Rumpschnickel said, "maybe he would." She had a stubborn, subdued courage, however; and finally she did join the Methodist Church. It was easy to join in secret, because Old Man was always downtown from ten to two and she was able to attend the eleven o'clock service and still get dinner on by two o'clock. She was happy and full of consolation after she joined the church.

This was all very well until the church began to ask for money. No church expected much in our town. The ministers had given up asking for a tithe, but there were certain maintenance expenses that could not be avoided.

Old Man never gave Mrs. Rumpschnickel or Eva a penny to spend without an accounting. If Eva wanted a whalebone stay for her Gibson Girl collar, she had to ask her father for a dime. And he would say, "Why do you need a blankety-blank whale bone for your blankety-blank collar? You look better without it." This was probably true, but still all of the girls in Eva's class had whalebone stays in their collars, and a girl's whole high school career can be ruined by a little thing like that. When Old Man said, "No!" Eva wept and Mrs. Rumpschnickel came to my grandmother.

My grandfather's death had left my grandmother with a little real estate and practically no money. She prided herself on being a business woman, however, so she got along pretty well by renting three small houses and raising her own chickens, vegetables, and fruits. But there was not much spare cash lying around. Yet she understood another woman's need and over the years she bought a lot of small commodities from Mrs. Rumpschnickel. She bought hand-made pot holders and sauerkraut and tidies for the chairs, and Eva had whalebone stays in her collars. But the church was another matter. Grandma contributed to the Presbyterian Church, and she could not afford to underwrite the Methodists as well.

At last there was one desperate day when Mrs. Rumpschnickel had to face her husband and tell him that she had joined the Methodist Church. You could hear him shouting for two blocks, cursing and blaspheming in a very rich and redundant style. Grandma made me come indoors and she shut all the windows because she did not wish to have me contaminated. But, before she confined me, I heard him yelling, "I'm an atheist, by God! And you've gone and joined a blankety-blank church and made a blankety-blank monkey of me."

It took a long time for the neighborhood to quiet down, and Mrs. Rumpschnickel never did get her money for the church. The church had to take her as she was with only what dimes and nickels she could get by selling things to my grandmother. But she kept on going to church every Sunday, and perhaps the fact that they had the wife of an atheist was glory enough for the Methodists without more material compensation.

Eva wanted to go on to college, but, of course, there was no earthly hope of that, and so, after graduation from high school, she obtained a position as an operator with the telephone company. Old Man had never allowed one of the blankety-blank telephones in his house, but Eva had seen her friends talking to each other over the instrument in their own homes and she was delighted at last to be a part of something that the other girls had. She had a sweet voice and she was a good operator who never repeated the private conversations she heard. Everything would have been lovely for her except that Old Man made her hand her pay check over to him at the end of every month.

"Papa, can't I keep just a little of it out for myself?"

"No, you cannot. What do you think I am, a blankety-blank millionaire? When you've paid back all the blankety-blank investment I've put in you, we'll begin to talk about keeping something out!"

But, in spite of the fact that she had nothing to spend on fancy clothes, Eva looked very pretty in her plain black skirts and white shirtwaists. She had glossy black hair and a nice high color on her cheeks and lips. A young man from the insurance office next door to the telephone company began to walk home with her in the evenings after work. She used to say goodbye to him at the corner below our house and go on alone to her own home. We knew about him before Old Man did, and in fact Mrs. Rumpschnickel had taken Grandma into her confidence almost from the start. His name was Charles Olson, and he was good and honest and making enough for two. He was handsome also, and generous with candy and other gifts that could be given to a nice girl without offense. I enjoyed a good bit of this candy, as Eva and her mother did not like to leave it around where Old Man might see it and ask questions.

"Rumpschnickel never gave me a thing before we was married," Mrs. Rumpschnickel said. "He just told me the date and the time."

Two handsome young people of opposite sexes cannot walk home every evening for months without some complications. Charles and Eva began to take longer and longer to say goodnight on the corner below our window, and once I saw them holding hands. The day after that Mrs. Rumpschnickel came over and told us that they were engaged.

"But we don't know what to do," she said. "Rumpschnickel won't be paid for Eva's bringing up for another two years. They don't want to wait, and what are we to do?"

Grandma was not afraid of living dangerously, and she said, "You had better tell him, Mrs. Rumpschnickel."

So the next day the young man went on home with Eva and asked her father for her hand in marriage. If we had not seen them going on from the corner to her house, we would have heard it all anyway. Old Man began to yell like a stuck pig. You could hear him for two blocks.

"You can't get married until you've paid me back, you blankety-blank ungrateful girl," he shouted.

"Mr. Rumpschnickel," Charlie Olson said, "I'll pay you back for Eva's upbringing. I've got some money in the bank."

"You keep out of this, you blankety-blank young whipper-snapper, you—this is between me and my blankety-blank child."

Grandma took me in then and shut the doors and windows so I did not hear all of it. But Old Man did not give his consent.

However, Eva had a little of his own spirit. The next day she walked out of the house to go to work and she never went back. She and Charles were married as soon as they could get a license, and the Methodist minister performed the ceremony without her father's consent. But first he asked her if she was an atheist, and she said, "No."

"It was a lovely wedding," Mrs. Rumpschnickel told my grandmother, "even if she didn't have a veil and a white dress and a bouquet like I had always hoped for her. Even if she didn't have a father to take her down the aisle. Rumpschnickel wouldn't go, of course."

"Don't you think he's sorry?" Grandma asked.

"Not Rumpschnickel. He told her never to darken his door again, and he means it."

"That's too bad. And what about you?"

"Oh, I'll miss her. But I'm glad for her. If I never see her again, I'm glad for her."

I don't know what came over Old Man after that. Sometimes he didn't go down town until eleven o'clock, and sometimes he came back at one, sometimes at three. His belly stuck out as far ahead of him as ever when he stumped along, but his face began to look more sagging than mean. Maybe it was because he didn't get paid what he had coming to him, or maybe the house seemed empty after Eva had gone, but something went wrong with him. He didn't curse and blaspheme as much in public as he had before she ran away. He even started giving Mrs. Rumpschnickel fifty cents a week spending money. That was what really frightened her.

"He's sick," she said to Grandma. "He's really a sick man. But I don't dare call a doctor to him."

"Go right ahead," Grandma said. "Call a doctor. He can't do any worse than he has done."

"But there'll be a bill to pay. He won't pay it. I never had a doctor to pay for, even when Eva was born."

"He'll pay it," Grandma said, "if it's to save his own skin."

So one day when Old Man Rumpschnickel did not feel like going down at all, Mrs. Rumpschnickel ran to our house and used our telephone to call the doctor. She called Eva too, but Eva said, "No, Mamma. If I came, it would make him worse. He'd yell his poor head off. We better leave him be."

The doctor came and looked at him and it seemed he had some malignant thing in that great fat belly of his and he would only have a short time to live. He cursed the doctor up and down and called him a blankety-blank liar. And, when Mrs. Rumpschnickel begged him to see Eva and forgive her, he cursed both of them and said they were blankety-blank leeches who had never appreciated all he had done for them.

He got a little quieter in the last days, he ate the chicken soup Grandma sent over, and he raised his wife's allowance to seventy-five cents. Poor woman, she did not know how to spend it after so many years of doing without things, but finally she spent it on a red necktie for him. When he saw the necktie he threw it in the wastebasket and told her she was a blankety-blank fool.

But that was the beginning of the end for him. Too much anger had worn him out. His mind began to wander at the last and he shouted things that he never had before. Strange words came up from very far down inside him.

"Save me!" he shouted. "Oh, God, I'm going to hell. I see the fires all around me! Save me! Save me!" You could hear him shouting about hellfire for more than two blocks before he died. In the silence that came after the shouting, we all stood amazed. It was such a great surprise to us to know that all those years, when he had been crying out that he was an atheist, he had secretly believed in hell.

His wife took the red necktie out of the wastebasket and he wore it in his coffin. She and Eva came into a lot of money.

12

Rosa

OR A BRIEF period one summer Rosa Kulhanek took mandolin
lessons from my aunt. I suppose that Rosa and I were about
ten at that time and we had known each other slightly at school the
winter before.

Rosa climbed our hill on a Saturday afternoon carrying a shabby
old mandolin case that had evidently been handed down by other
generations of Kulhaneks, and for half an hour she was closeted with
my aunt. Sounds of wildly picked strings, exclamations of impatience,
and a reckless tremolo were heard. Then Rosa bounced out looking for me and sometimes we spent the rest of the afternoon together.

Rosa was one of the numerous children of the shoemaker who
had his shop on Main Street between Fourth and Fifth. The Kulhaneks lived behind the shop, shrieking and singing and laughing loudly
in what appeared to be a most satisfying family life. Rosa was something of a curiosity to me, as doubtless I was to her. I was a frail,
pale child with long blond hair and introspective interests, and Rosa
was a hearty extrovert. She had red cheeks and curly, short, brown
hair, and her brown eyes had flecks of red and gold in them that
made them appear to be burning with little fires. She wore a gold
cross on a chain swung jauntily around her neck. Her hands were
always hot and moist, and laughter bubbled noisily up and down inside her.

One afternoon, when the lesson was over, we began to hunt
for four-leaf clovers. It seems to me today that clover patches do
not produce so many handsome specimens as they did when I was
young. There used to be four-leaf clovers on every wayside plot,
and a sharp-eyed child could pluck her quota of good luck on almost
anybody's lawn. We had a particularly productive patch of clover in

our side yard, and Rosa and I squatted there, seeking our fortunes. The sun was warm and sweet, and, if one had nothing better to do on a Saturday afternoon, it was a pleasant occupation.

My eye for four-leaf clovers was deadly and very soon I had two beauties to exhibit. It took Rosa much longer to find her first one. Whatever she did she did fast, and now she covered the patch with much more speed than accuracy. It irked her to see me get ahead of her.

"But Rosa, you have to go slow and look sharp," I said. "You can't just tramp through the patch in a hurry."

"Oh, bother!" Rosa said, and went on looking in her own way. But presently she said, "I've got one. Look at this." She held a large, fine clover with three big round leaves and one small one. I was not surprised at this because four-leaved clovers by their very nature are irregular, and often the fourth leaf will be smaller than the others. Still this one looked strange to me. Each of the three large leaves was marked with a delicate white half moon like the half moon on a fingernail, but the fourth small leaf was plain green.

"Let's see," I said. Rosa handed me the stem with great good nature, but, as soon as I held it in my own hand, I could see that the fourth leaf had been picked from another plant and stuck onto this one with a dab of hot saliva. The game was utterly spoiled.

"Oh, Rosa!" I cried, "that isn't fair. You cheated!"

"What's the diff?" cried Rosa merrily. "It looks as good as yours, don't it?"

My Scotch-Presbyterian conscience was seriously disturbed. "But it's not right," I said. "It's like telling a lie—it's like—"

"So what?" said Rosa laughing. "I can make lots more of them. I can have as many four-leaf clovers as I want to have."

I tried to expostulate and explain. My soul cried out that right was right and wrong was wrong and never the twain should meet. Rosa looked at me with condescending pity.

"But it's all right," she said consolingly, "I can confess it to the priest, and it will be all right."

"Just the same—" I began. I was marshalling all of my moral precepts and telling arguments, but I could see that Rosa wasn't listening. She had begun to laugh again.

"Well, kiddo, I gotta go," she said. "See you next week."

She snatched up her shabby mandolin case and went bouncing and skipping down the hill. I was left all alone, sitting in the clover patch, with my Scotch-Presbyterian conscience stuck like a round white pebble in the middle of my gullet. It was a long Saturday afternoon.

13

Leddy

I SAT ON THE FLOOR in the parlor shooting marbles. She came in and saw me, sat down beside me, took out the new false teeth that were giving her pain, and began shooting marbles at them. Her second family called her Aunt Alice, but for us she was always and forever Leddy.

Dr. Francis J. Ledbrook and his wife Alice came from England to take over my grandfather's practice. After my grandfather's murder the tiny office stood empty for a long time and my grandmother, who desperately needed the money, was delighted to rent it. My grandfather had been a noisy and voluble man who was both loved and hated. Dr. Ledbrook was a very quiet man, a competent but not a public person. One or two people might love him extravagantly, but, until his tragedy, I think that no one hated him. He was a very religious man, earnest and responsible, a devoted Methodist and member of the choir. He was handsome in an inconspicuous way, with blond hair and moustache, and two large front teeth with a gap between which were as British as his accent. What had brought him halfway around the world to a small pioneer town in Idaho? Had some character flaw driven him so far from England? Or was it only the itch of the age that had kept men moving westward for a generation? This was about 1903, I should say, and Idaho still offered a last frontier.

Leddy never spoke about him and we had the delicacy never to ask, for his life in our town had ended in a spectacular tragedy. People said that he was mad, that he had a sinister hypnotic influence which lured a young girl to her doom. They heaped him with every sort of calumny. The facts seem to be simply that he fell desperately in love with the pretty, vivacious young daughter of the Methodist minister, and she with him.

Today it might have caused a minor scandal: "Married man falls in love with fellow choir singer." So what? A few weekends in a motel in a neighboring town and everything is forgotten. Wife never knows; minister father never knows; town is cheated of its scandal. But when Dr. Ledbrook fell in love with Winnie Booth, it was Romeo and Juliet with the added complication of a wife. It was virtue in the snares of sin. It was tragedy.

Sometimes I think that we cannot have tragedies anymore in our modern world. There is every kind of crime and disaster, more than ever before, but genuine tragedy requires moral values. It requires virtue and sin and a sense of guilt. These things have very nearly been lost to us. When Dr. Ledbrook loved and desired so very deeply, virtue and sin and guilt were at their peak as influences in society. Divorce seemed out of the question. To live in sin outside of wedlock was even more unthinkable. In either case his reputation and hers would be forever tarnished. But could they give each other up? Could the sun stop shining and the moon stand still? There was only one clear answer. Dr. Ledbrook and Winnie Booth went to a neighboring town and spent a night which I hope was one of ecstasy and not of guilt. The next day they were found dead of morphine overdoses.

But I did not set out to tell the story of Dr. Ledbrook and Winnie Booth. I have fictionized it in *Buffalo Coat,* and Moscow, Idaho, already remembers it without my help.

The one person who came off badly in all of this was Alice Ledbrook, the plain and unloved wife. I don't think that I ever saw a plainer woman. I hesitate to use the word "ugly," because that has unpleasant connotations; she was one of the dearest and quirkiest and most amusing persons in my childhood. She had a skin of strange translucent whiteness, beetling black brows over beady black eyes, a nose that suggested a modified snout, the gap between the front teeth, and straight black hair which she pulled up hard from her forehead and twisted into a round knot on the very top of her head. There was no artifice in her. She knew she was a homely woman and she made no bones about it. How many hours I have spent at her knee, sitting on an English carpet hassock, gazing spellbound at that unusual face while she read aloud to me!

After the tragedy she must have been crushed. She was an un-pretentious person and she probably understood that her husband might fall in love with someone younger and more beautiful – really beautiful. But that he should love so much that he was willing to die and see the beloved die! It must have been a hard fact to get used to.

I don't know how she and my grandmother got together, but they had been friends, and Gram must have gone to her as soon as she heard.

"Will you go back to England?"

"No. There is no one there I want to see. Not after this."

"Then what will you do?"

"Sell this house. Get a room somewhere. I don't know, I might as well stay here and live it down."

"Well, we have an extra room. You wouldn't be alone. There are just my daughter and me, and the dogs, of course."

"I like dogs."

"You could come and go as you like."

"I really don't have many friends. It is good of you to offer."

"Well, come then. We'd be glad to have you."

It must have been six or seven years that Leddy lived with my grandmother and aunt. She was there when I came, an odd little woman who could understand the calamity that had just befallen an odd little girl. She rented the guest room that was later so often saved for Aunt Ett and Uncle Ash.

Gram's house was a peculiar architectural jumble, a fantasy of my grandfather's more expansive moments. Now, when I dream of being in a house, it is almost always laid out on the plan of this house. I have lived in many other houses in my life for longer periods of time, but this is the psychological dream house. Sometimes it will be large; sometimes small. It may be fitted with fantastic embell-ishments, but basically the structure is Gram's house. Originally it had been a small, thick-walled pioneer dwelling with a large kitchen, a step-up dining room, and an upper bedroom reached by a dark enclosed staircase leading up from the kitchen. At various times there had been added to it a large, high-ceilinged parlor to the right of the dining room, then behind the parlor two bedrooms and a sleeping

porch. To the left of the dining room there was a narrow dark hall-
way leading to a modern bathroom, and off this little hall opened
a good-sized bedroom under an ornamental tower. The tower was
one of my grandfather's grandiose inventions. It was only one story
high, and its peaked roof stood out on the side of the old house like
a bandaged thumb. But the room inside was very pleasant. It had
three windows on three sides of the tower. The other side was open
to the room with its bed, dresser, washstand, and chairs. In the cir-
cular space between the windows stood Leddy's desk and chair.
There was also an armchair and the carpet hassock.

Leddy's things always fascinated me. They were not like the
American things I had grown up with. She had a passion for mot-
toes, ornamental calendars, and bric-a-brac. Here her space was
necessarily limited and I did not realize the full scope of her passion for odd small things until I visited her house many years later.
But I remember with pleasure the ornamental inkstand, the Venetian glass paperweight, and a funny little old woman made out of
a wishbone with many flannel petticoats. Among the petticoats was
a scrap of paper which said:

> Once I was a merry-thought
> Living in a hen.
> Now I am a little slave
> On which to wipe your pen.

"But what is a merry-thought, Leddy?"

"Why, it's a wishbone, lovey. In England we call them merry-
thoughts."

Her jewelry pleased me too. She wore the very plainest clothes:
high-necked white shirtwaists with long black skirts, long black coats,
and unadorned black turbans. But she had many wonderful rings:
opals and pearls and emeralds and garnets. She wore most of them
every day on her strangely white, smooth-skinned fingers. The ringed
fingers were usually busy with a silver tatting shuttle. She made
yards of tatting lace to trim handkerchiefs and petticoats. Some of
it was very intricate, done with fine thread several inches wide. My
aunt did tatting but never such lacy fantasies as Leddy made.

Among Leddy's jewelry was a marvelous breast pin from which
dangled tiny gold scissors, hammer, tongs, shovel, and rake, but her

watch chain was the envy of my childhood. She wore her watch tucked into her belt. It was attached to a long golden chain made up of many links woven together so that the whole thing slipped snake-like through one's fingers. I had a teacher once who wore gold beads. These were the ultimate for me until I saw Leddy's sinuous watch chain.

Leddy occupied herself by writing letters, taking walks, and doing good deeds. The good deeds were connected with bed-ridden old ladies, widows, orphans, and the poor. These charities often occasioned her walks, but, even if there were no good deeds to be performed, she walked several miles every day. I don't remember that I ever walked with her (I had my own affairs) but the dogs did.

We had two mongrel dogs: a black, pseudo-water spaniel and what could only be known as a yellow cur. They were my particular friends and companions, but I gladly shared them with Leddy. She kept a hoard of hard candies in a tin box in her room, and, when she was ready for a walk, she rattled the candies in the box. Dogs' ears are said to be more sensitive than ours. Anyway the dogs always heard, no matter in what part of the house they might be dozing. They leapt to their feet and rushed yelping to her door, first for a candy and then for a walk. She never allowed them into her room, only as far as the door.

Sometimes she tried to fool them by rattling the box, then pretending that she was putting away her hat and coat and had already been away without them. But they were not to be put off by such unimaginable deceit. They leapt about her barking and begging until she relented to take them with her. I don't know what the town thought of the widow of the notorious doctor-assassin striding out briskly in her rusty black with the mongrel dogs leaping and grinning around her, but to me it was a beautiful sight.

I was acquainted with the contents of the tin candy box too, and the thick, round, white peppermints that she kept in her desk drawer.

She wrote and received many letters. It seemed that she had an extensive and loving family in England, but, as far as I know, she never went back even for a tourist visit.

Every week a distant cousin sent her a little packet of religious tracts; these were something like our Sunday School papers. They were full of stories of dying children who, with a last brave speech, reformed a drunkard father: or others who had eaten too many sweets (alas! the hard candies and the peppermints) but, having suffered a stomach ache, renounced their gluttonous ways and gave their candies to the poor. I had some tentative inklings of literary taste because my father and grandfather had left us a good library so I was an enthusiastic reader. But, although I could read better by myself, I loved the social coziness of being read to. I would have listened to the dictionary and the telephone directory if anyone had chosen to read them aloud to me.

So I sat entranced hour by hour while Leddy read to me. When we had exhausted the English tracts she read to me from the Elsie Dinsmore books. She had a friend who owned the complete set (thirty-four, I believe), and was eager to lend them. I remember the tasteful maroon covers, letters in gilt, all exactly alike: *Elsie's Motherhood, Elsie's Widowhood, Elsie at Margate, Elsie's Grandmother.* We read them all. I hated Elsie Dinsmore. She was a senseless prig, but, oh, the pleasure of sitting at Leddy's knee, sucking her peppermints, and listening to her friendly voice as it droned on and on. Was I one of the orphans to whom she was doing a good deed? No, I think not. I would have known. I sensed that she was as content as I to sit there in friendliness and trust while the rain beat on the yellow leaves outside the tower windows, and the dogs shuffled around in the hall outside her door waiting for the summons.

When we moved to Spokane to keep house for my Uncle Don, Leddy came with us. We had become her family. She and my grandmother had seen each other through calamities that would have crushed lesser women. They did not discuss their tragedies, but they had their daily routines, their small jokes and humors. They used to laugh over the fact that Leddy had gone into a drygoods store to buy a couple yards of "Fruit of the Loom" muslin and had shocked the clerk by inadvertently asking for "Fruit of the Womb." We used to have a joke about the fact that she liked a variety of jams and jellies with her breakfast toast and would never allow a leftover dab to be thrown away. So sometimes her breakfast plate would be surrounded by five or six small dishes with leftover bits of jam in them. She and my grandmother used to tease each other humorously about the unattached old gentlemen in the neighborhood. Nobody ever thought that either of them would marry again.

So we were astonished and amazed when Leddy did.

As soon as we moved to Spokane, Leddy began to go to the Methodist Church. She had been a devoted Methodist at home, even after the tragedy of her husband and the minister's daughter. There the congregation knew everything about her, and if she had lived the scandal down, it was more to her credit than theirs. Here in a strange city, people accepted her for what she was without a painful past. In middle age her plainness was not so striking as it had been when she was younger. She was full of kindness and good deeds and a brusque sense of humor. She was liked.

When in a few years we decided to go back to the home town, we expected, of course, that Leddy would go with us. The dogs would go, the pony and the canary bird would go, and Leddy, who was so much a part of the family, certainly she would go.

"No," she said. "I love to be with you and I shall miss you. But I'm going to stay here. I'm going to be married."

"Married?" we cried. "But who? You never told us."

"Well, he's a widower with a big family, all grown now. He's a very nice old gentleman, and he wants me. He really does."

He really did. He was a fine-looking old gentleman and she fell quite naturally and happily into a large, warm family of married children and grandchildren who called her Aunt Alice instead of Leddy and gave her the love she had always wanted.

This might have been the end of the story, as far as I was concerned, but no, for every summer she invited me up to visit her and Grandpa Quilliam. It was one of my great delights to go. I went all by myself on the electric train, and at the station I saw her waiting. She was the same small woman with sharp black eyes under frowning brows and a screw of black hair like a handle on top of her head. She still wore the high-necked white shirtwaists, but the belt that separated the waist from the black skirt had a more squeezed-in look because she had begun to put on weight. The plump white hands were as shiny and smooth as ever; on them were the marvelous rings.

After brisk and friendly greetings she took me by trolley car out to the small suburban house where she and Grandpa had a garden and a few chickens; they kept a story-book house. We went in by the back door and the kitchen walls were ablaze with the calendars that used to be an important advertising medium in those days. One calendar presumably being enough, most people discarded the unwanted ones, but Leddy and Grandpa kept them for art's sake. There were the flamboyant seed catalogue calendars with impossibly beautiful flowers and vegetables; the bare-bosomed ladies from the ice cream parlor; the cunning children from the grocery store; and the wise old doctor, watching beside a child bedded on two chairs, from the drugstore. One spread out like an immense red and yellow fan; another unfolded at a touch like a little shelf displaying a barnyard scene in realistic perspective. Television has robbed us of this glut of gaudy calendars, and, dubious as the replacement is, we are probably better off.

Still Leddy's kitchen was a joy to me, neat as a pin, but at the same time gloriously ornate.

We sat down to supper in the dining room, just the three of us, as Leddy and Grandpa sang a blessing while we all held hands. Then there were cold meats and potato salad with homemade bread and three kinds of jam and pickles, all served on ornamental plates, as diverse and pictorial as the calendars. They drank very black English tea, which was diluted for me with rich cream into a strange and lovely drink such as no child ever tastes at home.

Grandpa was originally from the Isle of Man; his grave and courtly manners spoke of the old world. Two of his granddaughters became my good friends, and the one who remains is still a dear and trusted friend after more than sixty years. Recently she gave me a snapshot, showing Grandpa holding one of the great grandchildren, having Leddy beside him in a white shirtwaist and a black skirt with frowning brows and a screw of black hair on the top of her head—the only picture of her that I possess. My mind, however, is stocked with many.

In the course of my visits to them there were sometimes momentary awkwardnesses, because Grandpa's memory began to fail. He would ask the same question several times during the meal and receive the same answer with the same exclamations of wonder. But one could not be impatient with him since he was so sweet-tempered and serene. Leddy and I just answered him as if he asked for the first time, and we did not even exchange glances. We were all three quite comfortable and happy.

On the golden-oak sideboard, among many vases and figurines, was a tin box, and, yes, it contained hard candies. And there was a little dog named Gyp. In a golden oak china cabinet with curved glass sides was distilled the treasure of both their lifetimes. I recognized the Venetian glass paperweight, the ornamental inkstand, and the merry-thought penwiper, but Grandpa had added his bit: there were souvenirs from the world's fairs, trophies from various sporting events, shells from many seashores, curious rocks and crystals, a little china lady appeared to be dressed in the finest lace (but it was really only china and not lace at all), a cup imitated a ripe tomato with a green leaf for a saucer, a gilded nutshell was made into a little boat with a gilt paper sail while a large mock peanut upon examination disclosed a papier-mâché mouse. It was like stepping through the Looking Glass to open the cabinet and be allowed to handle its contents.

And then, when bedtime came, I slept alone in the splendor of the guest room. Leddy would come to see that I had everything I needed, and then she would wind up a music box that sat on a hassock by the bedroom door. It played a lively waltz tune that gradually grew slower and slower as the spring unwound until at last with a little gasp it ended in silence. I lay in drowsy awareness, thinking, "Isn't this nice? Isn't this nice?"

And I think now, as I remember, "Isn't it nice that Leddy had a happy ending?"

14

Strangers

IN THE SUMMER, I went all over the countryside on my pony. I went whenever I felt like it. Often I got up before breakfast, then rode away before Aunt and Gram were stirring. They never seemed to fear for me, since fear was an emotion that I rarely experienced.

There was one time, however, when I was frightened. That time I was on a bicycle, and a bicycle is much more vulnerable than a horse. For a few years we had lived in a nearby city where I was given a lovely blue bicycle. In the city I rode on the sidewalks with a friend who had a red bicycle. We called our bicycles "Blue Streak" and "Red Racer." But after I returned to my small country town, I rode my bicycle less often. The wooden sidewalks were bumpy; the country roads were rutted and dusty or slippery after a rain. On the whole, a horse was safer and more fun.

But one morning in summer, when the days were hot and dusty, I got up very early in the morning to ride my bicycle out to the cemetery. There was nothing morbid in this. The cemetery was in the country at the intersection of two roads. I could ride out by one road and return by the other, never repeating a part of the route, to be home in time for a hearty breakfast.

The dew was still heavy on the grass; the shadows were long and blue; the coming heat of the day was only a distant threat. No one had begun to stir in the town. The birds were the only living things making a clamor of praise and rejoicing.

I mounted my bicycle without waking anyone in the house and pedalled joyfully away, gloating over my aloneness in the glory of the morning. The town streets and sidewalks were easy, but the road into the country was rough and pitted. Dust lay thick in the wheel tracks. It powdered the wayside weeds and wildflowers. The creek, which was only a seasonal phenomenon, was now dry with tufts of blue lobelia growing in the cracked mud of its bed. There were wild roses blooming in the fence corners, as well as the purple flowers that we used to call sugar bowls when they were in bloom and old women when they went to seed, producing a miracle of long, slightly curly gray hairs. I suppose that there must be a proper botanical name for these flowers, but I've never come across one in any wildflower book.

I knew and rejoiced in all the wildflowers, the thistles and white daisies, the Black-eyed Susans and goldenrod. I rarely came back from one of my jaunts without some weedy trophy to put in a jar of water or perhaps to try to draw or paint. But this morning I pedalled along energetically in the cool air, bumping and sliding and feeling utterly adventuresome.

Then suddenly, when I was well out of town with not a living soul in sight, a man rose out of the dusty weeds by the wayside and stood looking at me. He was dirty and ragged, unshaven and unwashed. To me he looked like a mad man, very large and menacing. He must have been sleeping there by the roadside, and was startled by the sound of my wheels bumping along the road.

Neither of us spoke, but we stared at each other with wild eyes. He could have reached out a long arm and pulled me off my bicycle, but I pedalled on by, a small, receding figure, scared as a rabbit.

I have often thought of this fearful apparition. How had he been so desperate as to spend the night in the roadside weeds? Was I, a small, lone girl in a vast untenanted countryside, really in any danger from him? In memory he seems a frightful figure, standing large, dishevelled, dazed, against the gold of early morning.

We had many tramps at our back doors in those days. Men were out of work, wandering the countryside. It was past the days of Coxey's Army, but the I. W. W.s were abroad.[8]

My aunt never turned a tramp away without giving him something to eat. I don't know whether my grandmother would have fed them so zealously or not. She was practical and level-headed, and she believed that people who really wanted work could find it. My aunt was first of all a sentimentalist who always said, with a slight tinge of self-congratulatory unctuousness in her voice, "I never turn a man away because, no matter how many are undeserving, one among them may be worthy."

Some of our neighbors, who refused to feed tramps, said that the tramps put a secret mark on our fence posts or that they spread the word in the railroad-siding jungles so that each new vagrant coming to town knew where to go for a handout. Certainly they seemed to come first to our door.

My aunt must have lived a very dull and hopeless life—an imaginative spinster living alone with a practical mother and an orphaned niece. I'm sure that tramps broke the monotony of her existence and fed her imagination as she fed their empty stomachs.

One in particular excited her fancy. I remember him well. He was a very personable fellow, well shaven and clean, although his outer garments were shabby. He came to the back door and asked for food, offering to pay for it with work. My grandmother could use a man to split the wood that she burned in the great kitchen range where she baked her bread. She or my aunt usually split it themselves but today the tramp split it for her.

Meantime my aunt laid a clean cloth on the kitchen table and set out an ample meal. The tramp came in and washed himself fastidiously at the kitchen sink. He turned up his shabby shirt sleeves before he washed, and Aunt declared later that the long knit undershirt of the period, which was revealed when he turned up his sleeves, was of pink silk. He spoke very intelligently, in cultured accents, of politics and the weather, sat down at the table after carefully pulling up his shoddy trousers, and looked all around him for a napkin. Somehow my aunt had neglected to put one on the table.

"May I have a napkin, please?" he asked. Aunt was filled with mortification. She brought out one of the best large white linen napkins and placed it beside his plate.

"Thank you so very much," he said, unfolding it neatly across his knees. He cleaned his plate with relish while my aunt stood by like an awe-struck servant girl.

When he had wiped his mouth on the linen napkin he complimented her on the excellence of her cooking and asked if he might see the daily paper. In a trance of delight Aunt scurried to get it for him. He scanned it very quickly, looking for something. Whether he found what he was looking for or not, I do not know. He rose from the table with most civilized thanks, went down the walk and out the front gate, and vanished from our lives.

But ever afterward my aunt declared that he was a bank teller who had absconded with a large sum of money, or else a man who had murdered his wife in a sudden excess of passion and was running for his life. "The napkin and the underwear would prove it, if nothing else," she said. "He was a cultivated man."

I was often embarrassed by Aunt's excessive and very vocal sentimentality. She took up with people easily. The more humble they were, the more she sought to set them at ease by exaggerated kindness.

At one time an old Scandinavian woman named Olson came once a week to help with the housework. We had never before needed a cleaning woman, and I'm sure that Aunt and Gram employed her because they felt that she needed the small amount of money they could pay her more than they needed it themselves. Mrs. Olson was a tiny, troll-like woman with a face as full of wrinkles as a dried prune. In an excess of love and kindness my aunt took to calling her Lady Olson. This went on for a week or two. Then one day Mrs. Olson arrived in a rage and said that she would no longer work for us—that we were mean and unkind people. There was quite a scene. My aunt pled with her and asked what had we done.

"Vell," said Mrs. Olson, "you make fun of me. I t'ink it over two, t'ree veeks, den I get mad."

"But I never made fun of you, Lady Olson," cried my poor aunt on the verge of tears.

"No?" cried Mrs. Olson at the top of her lungs. "See. You do it again. I am no lady, so vy you call me 'Lady,' unless you make fun?"

My aunt's tears were useless. Mrs. Olson never came again.

My aunt had a heart of gold, but I blushed for her excesses. How many times have I stood with hanging head and shrivelling soul while she said to some total stranger in a drygoods store or on a street car, "This is my little golden-haired girl. Isn't she a darling?"

15

Childers' and Sherfeys'

THE TWO PLACES that I liked best on Main Street were Childers' Ice Cream Parlor and Sherfeys' Book Store.

The allure of Childers' was easy to explain; all the children loved its little metal tables and twisted wire chairs, its tall glasses of pineapple ice cream soda with straws, and its candy counter full of mouthwatering delights. Even my pony knew Childers'. He would trot amiably down Main Street until he came to Childers', then he would pull in of his own accord and wait for someone to go in to buy him a bag of peanut brittle.

But Sherfeys' to most children meant school supplies: Hummer tablets, number-two Eberhard pencils, books that cost money and that nobody wanted to read. I was the strange exception, a child who loved Sherfeys' and went there even when the teacher did not send me. The smell of new paper and printers' ink was perfume to me.

As I think of it now, Sherfeys' was not a large store for a town with a burgeoning university. It had a small show window beside the front door; inside, it ran back in a long, narrow room, lined with bookshelves to the ceiling; a counter on either side; cluttered tables in the center. I have a hard time today remembering how small it really was because when I was a child it seemed immense and the book-lined walls seemed to run to a vanishing point of perspective in a dark, hazy distance.

Mr. Sherfey was a round-faced, pink-and-white man, who stood behind the cash register with a faintly sad, far-away look in his eyes. He was always courteous, always helpful, always polite, but somehow belonging to another world or thinking other thoughts.

Mrs. Sherfey sometimes helped him in the store or sat at a desk in the balcony at the back of the shop to do accounts. She was a tall, gentle lady with the kind of long curved neck for which Annie Laurie was famous and which the artist, Charles Dana Gibson, had recently made popular. She looked very kindly over the tops of her glasses at suffering school children with lists of requests. Both of the Sherfeys had great patience and great calm. They lived in a pleasant region of their own somewhere on the side of Olympus.

I was a regular customer of theirs, always in need of the latest *Oz* or *Little Colonel* or *Five Little Peppers* book. They were used to me. But once I really shook their deep tranquility.

It had been a dull summer, and somewhere I had gotten a catalog full of brief book reviews. I was probably eleven, going on twelve. I marked the books that appealed to me and I counted up quite a tidy sum of accumulated allowance. Books were fortunately cheaper in those days, and even moderately low-income children could afford to buy them. I'm sorry for children now, book prices being what they are.

When I had studied and marked and figured, I decided that I could afford seven books. Great magic lay in the fact that I had selected them myself out of a catalog. I walked downtown and presented my list of seven books to Mr. Sherfey.

"But we don't have any of these in stock," he said.

"I know," I said, "but I would like to have you order them for me, please."

"But there are *seven* of them," he protested.

"I know," I replied confidently.

He looked at me very strangely. It was the first time that I had ever seen him jolted out of his calm. None of my earlier purchases had quite prepared him for this.

"Excuse me," he said. "Just a moment, please."

He went to the back of the store and climbed the stairs to the balcony. Mrs. Sherfey rose from her seat at the desk and I was aware that they looked down on me from above. I was sorry to disturb them and a little embarrassed to be buying more books than the "regular" children bought. Still I knew what I wanted.

They conferred silently, and then I saw Mrs. Sherfey nod her head. Mr. Sherfey came downstairs to face me across the counter.

"You're sure you wanted seven?" he asked.

"Yes," I replied. "I've saved my allowance. I can pay you for them." I always had the confidence of a person of independent means. A generous allowance was doled out to me every week, and I knew that it came from my own money and that more was in the bank.

"Very well," Mr. Sherfey said, but his hand shook as he wrote the order. He had had a hard shock.

I waited with impatience for several weeks, but finally I was notified that the books had arrived. I hitched up the pony and drove down Main Street with anticipation. The pony would have enjoyed stopping at Childers' but I kept a tight rein as we went on to Sherfeys'.

Mr. Sherfey was very pleasant today. He had a warm gleam in his eye, as one bibliophile greeting another bibliophile. The box was quite a sizable one and he helped me load it into the back of the pony cart. I drove home with all the speed that the pony would put forward to be alone with my treasure. I was not disappointed. The books smelled gloriously of new paper and printers' ink. They were totally undistinguished fiction books, not a classic nor an educational book among them.

There was an odd thing, however. One book I could not remember having ordered. It was a squarish book with a bright green cover and it was called *Juan and Juanita*. It proved to be a very dull story for young children, but it had nice illustration. Considerably puzzled, I re-counted my books. Yes, there were only seven. How then had I come by *Juan and Juanita?* In my mind I went over the titles I had selected, and one was missing. *Juan and Juanita* was a substitution for *Three Weeks* by a lady named Eleanor Glyn.

So I have gone through my life without ever reading *Three Weeks*. But on the whole I was satisfied. I had had my fling.

Once, returning early from a trip while our house was still rented, we lived for a short time next door to the Sherfeys. Mr. Sherfey preserved his Olympian detachment, but I became better acquainted with Mrs. Sherfey and with the excellent quality of her cookies. What I liked most and remember best about their house was a sofa cushion on their parlor settee. It was made of pink net, filled with little scraps of paper on which something had been written.

"You see," Mrs. Sherfey said, looking gently at me over her glasses, "Mr. Sherfey and I had a long courtship and wrote each other many letters. We saved them all, and, after we were married, we tore them up into little bits and made this cushion of them."

I was impressed. Through the pink net I could make out many words: "borrow," "percent interest," "marriage would be possible," "a small shop," "we can hope." But I was a romantic child, and, by shifting and shaking the torn bits of paper, I eventually came upon "millions of kisses," and with patience pieced together the scattered bits, "darling," "love you," "forever". . .

16

Two Beautiful People

ALL OF US children knew Miss Robinson, who taught the third grade. "Good morning, Miss Robinson," we said, knowing that, when we met her in the hall on a winter morning, she would have a smile for us. She was young and so blond, so pretty, so kind, that a smile from her started the day well. Some of the older children, who knew about such things, wondered why she was not married, because in our day all pretty young ladies were early married.

But it seemed that there were difficulties at home for her. After all these years I am not quite clear what these difficulties were. It may be that her mother was dead and that she was the eldest of a line of children. Certainly she had a way with children, and somehow she had responsibilities beyond her years.

Her father was the town clerk, a respectable man, if a trifle corpulent. Gram, according to her custom of speaking disdainfully of other corpulent persons although she was fat herself, called him "Old Fatty Robinson" when she saw him walking down the street. But her nickname was never quite as scathing as when she spoke of "Old Fatty Rumpschnickel" or other waddling persons.

People thought well of the Robinsons, although they were not on the upper rungs of our social ladder. Mary Robinson was not invited to the parties that were given in the social end of town. Prewar England could not have been more strictly regulated according to a system of social castes than our town at the turn of the century. We had an aristocracy which included the bankers and the most suitable families in the upper branches of trade, such as merchants, jewelers, implement dealers; also the most eligible doctors and lawyers and their families; and the livelier members of the university faculty.

For a time my own family had hovered on the edge of this local aristocracy, but misfortune and scandal and lack of money had brought us to the next level of caste, the unsung middle class who attended to business but rarely went out socially. The Robinsons belonged to our unheard majority, and such social life for them probably came through neighborhood or church connections. Below this there were other castes: the good people of "Swede Town," the pool hall and saloon habitues, the plumbers and gravediggers. No one was on relief.

The university on the hill across town was quite young in those days. Northern Idaho politicians and enthusiastic local citizens, of which my grandfather was one, had pulled strings to get the state university for our town. That it was isolated and inaccessible from the southern part of the state where the seat of government was located, mattered to none of them. The great idea was to get the university at any price. And so we finally had it, on a lovely hill looking across the town and the rolling wheat fields to the blue mountains beyond. The legislators in the south never saw it in the light of local pride in which we viewed it. North and south in our state were separated by a barrier of mountains, and a student from the south had to go through two adjacent states in order to attend his university. It is a wonder that the university ever survived its infancy to become a respectable and, indeed, a distinguished institution.

By 1900 the struggling university had had two presidents and was ready to welcome a third. There had been much dissention and discontent during the regime of the second president, and the regents were warily considering a number of eligible men. They particularly liked the looks of James MacLean, a thirty-two-year old Canadian of Scotch-Irish descent, who was six feet two inches tall, dark and handsome except for incipient baldness, and already a scholar of some note.

When he was interviewed, he said bluntly: "There are three reasons why I should not be invited to the university as its president. I am a bachelor so I would be handicapped in entertaining, I am a Canadian, and I smoke." Smoking was then a cardinal sin, but the regents forgave him that. They forgave him the fact that he was a Canadian, and they winked at each other over the first objection.

"Bachelorhood can always be cured, Doctor," they said. "We'll take a chance on you."

There were dozens of ladies willing and eager to assist the new president with his social obligations. The town's aristocracy turned itself inside out to be obliging to such a forthright and handsome young man in such an enviable position. Particularly mothers with marriageable daughters put themselves out to be agreeable to President MacLean. He was delightful to everyone. He went to the parties and made himself charming, but it was soon apparent that he had come to run a university and not to look for a wife.

The university had a fine new administration building erected in the grandiose manner of the late 1890s. There was a high central tower with much ornamental red and white brickwork as it stood on a big rolling campus of some twenty acres that had recently been a wheat field. Behind this imposing facade there was a small, ill-paid faculty and practically no funds for further development.

President MacLean set out to improve the faculty, to raise money, to enlarge the library, to encourage new students, and to make a decent educational institution out of a pioneer dream. He became a kind of hero in our town. As a small child I remember quite well his tall, dark good looks, his attractive combination of friendliness and dignified aloofness. Everybody courted him, but no one seemed to be preferred above anyone else.

Six years after he came to the university as its president, when the big administration building caught fire on a windy night and burned to an empty, blackened shell, it seemed that his career and that of the infant university were over. It was such a dark time that he told people later he used to find himself walking the streets with tears in his eyes. In the midst of such a vast calamity to the town there was a surge of loyalty and affection for the lonely man who had been pushing the university toward a rosy future. Now he paused, took stock, and began to make new plans and hunt for new funds. His innovations and bold ideas tided over the most difficult time. He began to build again, and the new buildings were more appropriate than the old. Out of the ruins he pulled a new and better university. But the town saw his loneliness and wished very much to allay it.

"If only he had a wife to console him," the important people of town said as all of their daughters were willing to undertake the role of consoler. He was invited to more and more dinners and dancing parties. He was plied with food and drink, with kind-hearted matrons always maneuvering him into corners with eligible young ladies. Somehow nobody ever thought that he might be looking around for himself. If they had suspected that he was, there would have been some general consternation.

During the long summers I used to ride my pony all over the Idaho hills. No one worried about me. I used to be gone half the day, all by myself, jogging between dusty hedgerows and rail fences, climbing the hills to the place where the pines crowded out the wheat fields and looking back over the little town where so many interesting things were going on. I was curious about every tree, every flower, and how the seasons turned. I knew the animals I saw along the way; I could name the birds and recognize their songs. But, although I loved the country, I respected the town, and in the final count it was the town's people who interested me most.

And one day as I rode along beside the cemetery I saw two people half reclining in the long grass among the wildflowers. They were holding hands. I was so much surprised that I did not even draw rein but rode quietly on by; probably they did not even know that I had passed. But I see them very clearly still: the tall dark man leaning toward the pretty blonde girl, telling her something very earnestly. All about them the long grass moved gently in the mountain air while the yellow wildflowers swayed and nodded.

How the two people got there I do not know because I saw no horse or carriage. And how had they escaped the vigilant eyes of the town to find a quiet moment for courtship? How, in fact, had they ever met at all? It was very wonderful.

So I counted myself the first to know (before the ambitious mothers and the hopeful daughters, before the socially prominent and well-to-do fathers, before the board of regents and the members of the faculty, before the ever-curious and gawping townspeople), that President MacLean was going to marry Mary Robinson. But it was so, as suddenly one day they were married to the consternation and amazement of everybody — except to a young girl on horseback.

They say that Mary MacLean, soon after her marriage, announced that she hoped to have eleven sons so they could have their own family football team. Actually they had six sons, only enough for a hockey team—but then, he was a Canadian. Just before I entered the university, President MacLean left to become chancellor of the University of Manitoba in Canada. They are all gone now, but I still see two beautiful people, lost in each other's eyes, lying on a grassy bank in an eternal summer.

17

The Boy Next Door

WHEN I WAS growing up in Idaho the summer nights were full of smells and sounds. The odor that lingers longest is that of the honey locust tree in blossom just outside the little screened porch where I slept. The sound was the piano-playing of the young man who lived next door. In winter he was away at college or his playing was shut inside the dark house behind its evergreens while I was snugly indoors.

But late in the summer night, long after I had gone to sleep and reawakened with moonlight on my face, the piano playing went on: ambitious, passionate, yearning, determined. It always filled me with sadness which I can in no way explain, except that it reminded me of my mother. The sound of a distant piano, at night, in the open air, still fills me with this nameless sorrow, something too lonely and pitiful to bear.

The house next door belonged to a family of three by the name of Desportes. The father of the family was a short, stocky French Canadian. He had something to do with the lumber business and he traveled a great deal. Small and intense, he bristled and crackled with energy and purpose. When he was at home his loud voice echoed through the quiet house, the lawn mower whirred, doors banged, people came and went. When he was gone, the house fell silent, the lawn was unmowed, no one came or went. Then Mrs. Desportes, in mid-morning with a coffee cup in her hand and a long wrapper over her nightgown, walked gently, serenely among the flowers in her backyard.

She was a good friend of my grandmother's, although they rarely stepped inside each other's house. But on these sunny mornings, when she took her coffee cup into the backyard, they used to talk over the back fence with pleasure and a mutual appreciation. There was much over-the-back-fence gossip in our town, but my grandmother and Mrs. Desportes rarely gossiped. They talked about the flowers and how the cherries on their trees were ripening and what was the best way of making cherry jam, and would it rain tomorrow. I stood by, bright-eyed and listening, but nothing they said was worth remembering. Only it was good to stand there in the sunshine, feeling the warmth and friendliness, feeling there was time for everything.

Mrs. Desportes was a very tall, thin woman, beautiful in a vague, emaciated way. Her high-arched nose gave her a bird-like appearance. Her hair was dark and curly; her eyes gray and wide with intensely black pupils. Although she was gentle, there was a strange effect of wildness in her eyes, the wildness of surprise or innocence or perpetual wonder. She moved very slowly, drifted it seemed, like a petal or a snowflake on a scarcely noticeable breath of air. She smiled a slow smile, and, when she talked, she used her hands in vague, gentle motions.

Somehow between the two of them, this strange couple had produced a son. He was short like his father and very slight. He had some of his father's nervous energy and drive, but the dark curly hair, the high-arched, bird-like nose, the wide gray eyes filled with the wildness of surprise came from his mother.

Quite early in life Louis Desportes decided to become a musician. His father was equally determined that his son should follow him in the lumber business. We heard only the back-fence echoes of the battle that went on in the house next door. When the father was at home the piano was silent; but there was shouting and cursing and a noisy "laying down of the law." When he was absent, the piano was heard from morning to midnight, and the mother walked in the garden with her coffee cup, gently smiling. I cannot think that she ever raised her voice in the family debate. She must have stood between the two men, hoping for the best, believing that each man must decide his future for himself. But under her softness, I think she was steady as a rock.

It was a gloomy, narrow house in which they lived. It stood nearer the street than our house did, but a row of dark trees hemmed it in and set it apart. It was painted an ugly brown. One delightful thing—among the evergreens there was a mulberry tree that used to drop its purple fruits on the sidewalk. I taste them yet. This was the first mulberry tree that I had ever seen, and it interested me greatly because I had read about the silkworms of China and how they fed on mulberry leaves. Idaho seemed to me so remote from all the gaudy things I read in books that I was delighted when I found something on my home street that linked me with the romantic world beyond our Palouse hills.

Louis's music, too, was something strange and exotic in a town of lumberyards and dusty board sidewalks. Secretly I hoped that he would win his battle with his father.

The Desporteses had little daily contact with the town. Mrs. Desportes telephoned the butcher and the grocer, and delivery boys brought what she needed. She rarely went out. The son attended college in a town nine miles away.[9] Mr. Desportes, small, virile, with an appreciative eye for large women, was so often away that local people scarcely knew him. For all we knew he may have had other menages in other towns where he hung his hat during his long absences. Something about his cocky masculinity no doubt inspired these idle speculations.

Drama of any sort was quickly sensed by the town. There was no television or radio, and the moving pictures were so new and inexpert in their interpretation of life that we needed our neighbors' drama to give us excitement. So, although few knew the Desporteses intimately, the town took sides in Louis's struggle with his father. Most of the town aligned itself with the father. Even my grandmother shook her head and wondered how a musician was likely to make a living. And did the boy next door have enough genius and determination to fight through to a successful career?

So we watched with interest and attention, but there was no dramatic moment of decision to gratify us. In time the most pliant drops of water will wear away granite, and, at some point in the long discussion, Mr. Desportes must have shrugged his shoulders and spread his hands in the Gallic gesture of resignation. Louis would become a musician.

"He'll never make it," most of the townspeople said. It would be nice if I could say how wrong they were.

We had little experience in judging musicians. We knew what we liked and Louis's music sounded all right to us. It was certainly classical and too far beyond us for criticism. He would not debase himself by playing in the local moving picture palace where we might have understood him better. Other local musicians were glad enough to get the movie palace job. My wilder aunt held down this job for some time with great success. She played by ear, and, watching the silent screen, would suit her music to the rhythm of the film. She was very good at improvising appropriate transitions. But Louis would not prostitute his act.

He let his curly black hair grow a little longer than we were accustomed to see in men, and, when he played in public, he had all the mannerisms which we associated with the classics. He twirled the piano stool to an exacting height, and then he rubbed his hands together silently before he began, raising his eyes toward the heavens for inspiration. He lifted his hands high before they crashed down on the opening chord, and his dark hair fell in disorder over his forehead. He was the perfect picture of a musical genius. We began to feel civic pride in his performance.

After he finished college we saw less of him. He went to a nearby city to complete his education. We were used to losing our ambitious young people to the larger sphere of the city. Minnie Robeson, a regal beauty, tall and amply developed, had also gone there to complete her vocal training with a view to an operatic career. There were many others.

Mrs. Desportes still wandered among her flowers carrying her coffee cup on a sunny morning, and, over the back fence, we had occasional news of Louis. He had given a concert at the First Methodist Church; he was taking a few selected pupils; he had composed a song and was looking for someone to sing it.

"Why doesn't he look up Minnie Robeson?" Grandma suggested. "She's there to learn to be an opera star."

"He doesn't know her," said Mrs. Desportes.

"Well, tell him to look her up. They're both from our town."

The next we heard Minnie was singing his song at a concert in the Odd Fellows Hall and after that in the Dunkard Church, and then they gave a joint concert for the Ladies' Cultural Society in the Elks Temple. It was only a step after that until they were married. It seemed that Louis had inherited from his father, along with his small stature, an appreciation for large and florid women.

"I wish I could have been at the wedding," Mrs. Desportes said, "but it was all quite sudden. They never told us until it was all over. I was pleased, of course, but Desportes was quite upset. He doesn't know how they are going to get along financially without his help."

Some time after this the town was edified by the announcement that Mr. and Mrs. Louis Desportes would give a musical entertainment in the First Presbyterian Church. We dressed in our best clothes and went to hear them. The church was full of people, not necessarily music lovers, but those who had predicted that Louis would never make it and friends of the bride who felt that she had thrown away her career by marrying so young.

Louis was the same, only a little more so. His hair was a little longer and he flung it more wildly. He twirled the piano stool more times and lifted his hands higher. We were so busy watching him that we may not properly have attended to the sounds he made. It was all very classical.

And then the bride appeared for her first number. She was really beautiful with large dark eyes and dimples. Except for the dimples she would have made a fine Valkyrie. She wore a long pink satin dress and she sang very well, at least we all thought so. She sang Louis's song, and it was something about butterflies and daisies and love, but it was over so soon that we scarcely realized that we had heard it. The least we had expected was something like Robert Schumann or Carrie Jacobs Bond. We expected roast beef and we were served a small eclair. For her final number she sang "The Last Rose of Summer," holding a long-stemmed pink rose in her hand, and, as she sang she slowly tore off petal after petal and dropped them onto the floor. Only the stalk was left as she ended her song. We burst into wild applause.

Am I laughing at them? And if so, I wonder why? If they had gone on to stardom I would remember all of this more reverently, thinking how lucky I was to witness the beginning of celebrity. But there was more pathos than we knew in the scattered petals. For all their trying neither young artist became great. In a couple of years their marriage ended in divorce. The concert stage did very well without them.

I grew up and moved away, married and busied myself with my own life. I rarely thought of Louis Desportes, except sometimes when I heard a piano played at night, and then I was filled with the old sadness. I thought, "He must have had something, some very small divine spark to put such permanent feeling in me. I wonder what has become of him?" But the thought did not linger long enough to make me inquire.

I don't know when his mother ceased to walk among the flowers with her cooling coffee, nor when his father surrendered up his cocky virility. Years later, when I went back for a visit, other people lived in the house. It had been painted white and most of the gloomy evergreens had been cut away. The mulberries were gone. Even my grandmother's house was irrevocably changed. I could hardly recognize our street. How futile it is to try to go back to any childhood home. The only unchanging scene is in one's own mind and it is always available without an airplane ticket.

I have been lucky enough to have a small success in my own career. When Louis Desportes was dreaming of the concert stage I was already dreaming of becoming a great writer. I have settled for much less than greatness. But it did happen one year that I was autographing books in Chicago, and that my name was in the paper in this connection.

Among the strangers who paused by the table where I sat in the book department of a leading store I was suddenly conscious of a familiar face. The curly dark hair had a few threads of gray, but, above the high-arched, bird-like nose, the wild gray eyes were as innocently full of wonder as they had ever been. He had not acquired a wrinkle or a fretful line.

"Louis Desportes!" I said. I felt immeasurably older than he was.

"The little girl next door!" he cried. "Think of that! And you knew me! You remembered me!"

We shook hands and he asked me if he could see me at my hotel later. He came promptly and stayed a very long time. I was tired, but I tried not to show it. He was full of talk about the "good old days in Idaho." I had scarcely exchanged a word with him in the "good old days," but now the accident of our having lived next door to each other made us boon companions. I couldn't help sensing the emptiness of a life that made these slender past relations seem important to him. I think too that he was warming his hands at my small success. He was pleased that I had made it, and he told me at length how many, many times he had nearly made it himself. His musical setting of the Lord's Prayer had come out simultaneously with one composed by a better known man with more influence. The concert agency had almost booked him for a season's tour but some one with a greater reputation had barged in and taken the job away. The University of Chicago had considered hiring him to teach in their music department but there was jealousy among the members of the department and someone had blackballed him. He had hoped at least that he might get a position at his alma mater in the West, but they had a full staff and no money for extra appointments; they had written him a lovely letter. The leader of a local dance band had wanted to hire him as the pianist, but of course a job like that was beneath his notice.

"But how do you get along?" I asked.

"Oh," he said, "I have a few pupils, and I expect at any time that something good will present itself. I like to keep myself free for the big-time offer. And my wife teaches in a girls' school."

"Your wife?" I repeated, seeing in my mind's eye the large, dark-eyed beauty dropping her rose petals as she sang.

"Yes," he said. "I'm married again to a wonderful woman. Edna, her name is. She would have been here with me today, but, of course, she is busy at school."

Later I met the second Mrs. Desportes. She was tall and stately, but she was neither Brunhilde nor Mimi.

"No, I'm not a musician," she said. "I'm just a plain school teacher but I love music, and it is so wonderful to feel that I can be a help and inspiration to a man of Louis's genius." I am sure that she believed sincerely in his genius, as he believed that only quirks of fate had kept him from a meteoric career. They were both happy in their beliefs. I saw no doubts or envy in them. At any moment the big break might come.

After that I received a Christmas card from them every year, and usually Louis would pen in a few bars of music which he had composed especially for me. Mrs. Desportes would ask about my books. In a year when I did not have a new book she would remark that she had been reading all the reviews in vain and had not seen my name. It was almost as if she reproached me for failing them in their vicarious expectations. One day they called me up from our own city, and I invited them to dinner.

"We are looking up our best old friends," they said, "and you are one of the best. We're on our way back to Louis's college for his twentieth class reunion."

"I want Edna to see all the dear familiar places and faces," Louis said. "It's a pilgrimage into the past."

"You'll find it very much changed," I warned. But they were happy in their illusions, and perhaps Louis's roots had never gone so deep that he would notice the changes.

After dinner he played for us. We had a piano bench that would not suffer adjustment, and, for lack of use, our piano was out of tune. But he made the best of it, rubbing his hands together and gazing skyward for inspiration. He lifted his hands high and came down crashing on the opening chord. His long dark hair, now threaded with silver, fell across his forehead. It was just the same as it had been before. The change was not in Louis but in me. I had listened to much music in the years which intervened between the concert in the First Presbyterian Church and that moment. I was a woman grown, but the boy next door was still the boy next door.

"Isn't he wonderful?" Edna said softly.

"Yes," I said. "Yes, he is." I meant what I said. To have preserved that boyish confidence and innocent optimism! It was a remarkable achievement.

"I was so lonely before I met Louis," she said quietly. "It seemed as if my life had no purpose. But now I have the privilege of doing for him and helping him with his career. I can't tell you how much it means to me."

They returned with glowing accounts of the twentieth reunion. They had gone to our home town and looked up all the prominent people. Louis had first-name news of this and that important person. I was sure that he had hardly known them in the "good old days," but they were all his friends now, at least he thought so, and Edna was breathless with the thrill of it.

Was it all pretense? Did they have silent moments together when they faced the fact that Louis had not succeeded in his career, that it was only Edna's school teaching that kept them off relief, that most of their friends were merely acquaintances bound to them by the slenderest of ties? I have often wondered. This is a story without a climax. So many real-life stories are. After the promising beginning, the road begins to slant downhill; there is really nothing to tell without the aid of fiction.

A few years ago I had a pathetic letter from Edna telling of Louis's death.

"He was so young still, so promising," she wrote. "I will dedicate my life to preserving his memory."

There must have been life insurance, and she had only one to support now on her salary. She scraped together the funds to endow a musical scholarship in Louis's name at his old college. She went out to be at the commencement when it was first bestowed. She was surrounded by Louis's friends. She traveled in her vacations from the school, and she sent me postcards. But her letters and cards were always sad. She was trying to be brave and find new interests, but the light of her life was gone.

The last letter I had from her was filled with plans for a year's study in England, and I thought that her time of mourning had run out, that she would soon be looking forward again. I sent her the usual Christmas letter, but I had no word from her. There are so many cards at Christmas that I really did not miss this one.

But then along in January I had a letter from a stranger:

"I am a fellow teacher at Edna's school. I have had the sad duty of going through her Christmas cards and notifying her friends of her untimely death. It has been a great tragedy for us that she should take her own life. It seemed she did not find her life worth living without her husband."

When I hear the lonely notes of a piano played at night, I think of them: what is success and what is failure?

18

Aunt Et and Uncle Ash

MY GREAT AUNT ET, Henrietta Woodhouse Pierce, was a hand-some woman, or at least she seemed so to me. She was not pretty, but she was tall and statuesque and superbly and proudly carried her head and shoulders. Her bright red hair was combed up neatly into a round pompadour, and she had a perpetually amused look about the mouth and eyes as if she judged the world critically and sardonically, finding it tolerable and diverting.

I remember seeing her naked once through the crack of a half-opened bedroom door. She and my uncle Ash were staying with us on one of their long visits and I had to go late to the bathroom, which was next to the company bedroom. I had no intention of spying and I was alarmed to find myself in the position of a spy, but I think that they never knew that I had been there. My great aunt was quite white and shapely, a fine figure of a woman, and I was shocked to realize that husbands and wives saw each other naked and perhaps liked it that way—even old people like great aunts and uncles.

There were no men in our household, except when Uncle Ash came to visit, and I was extremely unlearned in what is now so openly discussed in front of every child. "Sex" was a word that no one used freely when I was young. I think that the relationship between men and women was more glamorous at that time, because it was more mysterious and it was still associated with love. Sex today has become very unlovely, as it has been clinically dissected and exhibited in all of its strange manifestations. We are better off knowing less and imagining more.

I'm sure that Aunt Et must always have been attractive to men. She had two husbands, and an old story of her girlhood has always pleased me. My grandmother used to laugh and tell how Hetty, as she was called then, had a great admirer in one of the young farm hands. He had a fine red shirt of which he was proud. One day during a summer thunder shower, Hetty, in a clean white dress, ran to the barn to get some potatoes that were stored there. The men who had been working in the fields were obliged to take shelter from the storm, and the red-shirted admirer had found his shelter in the barn. Hetty was gone a long time, and, when she came sauntering unconcernedly back with her basket of potatoes everyone in the house could see that she had a broad red band across the back of her white dress just where an arm had been. Well, colors are fast now and sex has been psychoanalyzed.

Aunt Et's first husband was named Will. I have forgotten his last name and I never saw him. He was the brakeman on a railroad train, and he was killed in a railway accident while she was still quite young. For all of her ample charms, she had never had any children. But she liked children, and she knew how to please and entertain them. She stood for no nonsense, but she and Uncle Ash gave me many happy hours, teaching me things that I would not have learned from Gram or Aunt Elsie.

With only a husband and no children Aunt Et had had time to cultivate the arts. She played the piano and sang. I still see her, erect and stately, sitting before our old upright piano, accompanying herself as she sang:

> Mrs. Wealthy has her jewels,
> None have I,
> Mrs. Wealthy has her carriage,
> None have I . . .

I cannot quote the rest of it, but it was something to the effect that "I, like Cornelia, had my children," and that "these were my jewels." There was irony and perhaps wistfulness and regret in this favorite song of a childless woman. Her voice was deep and rich with a sort of hollow resonance that carried over into her measured speaking tones. What she said was not so much a comment as a pronouncement. The voice made all the difference, and, when she said, "I must get a new spool of thread," you felt that she had uttered a weighty and well-considered truth.

She did all sorts of embroidery, crochet, tatting, quilting, any-thing that was then called fancy work, and I still have bits of it after all these years. When she was middle-aged, she took up china paint-ing. Entirely self-taught and innocent of the traditions of art, she became extremely proficient at painting flowers, leaves, fruit, and all sorts of natural objects on plates, pitchers, bowls, vases, cups, saucers – on anything made of china. Her taste was absolutely cath-olic; she did not discriminate. For years we had a lemonade pitcher on which she had painted very realistically the stump of a giant red-wood with a carriage drive cut through it. It was so ugly that I used to shudder to look at it. But then, on the other hand, she painted most exquisite platters with flowers and fruit done with such skill and charm that they won prizes whenever she entered them in com-petition. She did not seem to know which were beautiful and which were not. She painted what she saw and what was pleasing to her at the moment.

Aunt Et was fond of animals. She and Uncle Ash always had one or two little black and tan dogs. How many Crickets or Gingers they had, I don't know, but there was always, it seems to me, a tiny black and tan terrier with watering eyes sitting and shivering on the broad, stately lap of my great aunt.

Aunt Et and Uncle Ash moved more often than any other peo-ple I knew. They would settle in some obscure Western town with an intriguing name (Pasco, Kennewick, Whidbey Island, Snoqualmie Falls), then Uncle Ash would open a jewelry store. Sometimes they would live behind it or they would have a small house. They never lived *above* the store because Aunty had a deep affinity with the earth; she had to have a garden. They would cultivate the garden and fur-nish the house. Even if it were only a large room behind the store, the home would take on an air of friendliness and permanence and timelessness. But then in a few years Uncle would be restless and they would pack everything and find a new odd-sounding town and move there.

As a child I did not understand these moves. I simply took them for granted. I'm not sure that I completely understand them today. They had something to do with the fact that Uncle Ash was a poor businessman, that he enjoyed giving expensive gifts, and that every so often he stepped "off the wagon" and had a wild encounter with the bottle.

Between one odd-sounding town and another they would come to visit Sister, as they called my grandmother. Once they even tried our town for a couple of years, but it was no more steadying for them than any of the others. Their visits were never deplored but were eagerly anticipated. Aunty helped about the house and Uncle gave us lavish gifts, and their company was always delightful. I never saw Uncle Ash when he was on the bottle; I saw him as an infallibly lovely gentleman.

He was tall and extremely thin, with a bristling moustache and rather wild blue eyes behind glasses. When I picture Don Quixote to myself, he looks like Uncle Ash. There was a touch of Cyrano de Bergerac in him too. The nose was not so large, although it was definitely there, but I could easily imagine Uncle laying about him with a rapier while he improvised a sonnet. He treated us all with beautiful tact, joshing Sister Caddie to put her in good humor and delighting my unmarried aunt with romantic gallantry.

He won my heart by speaking to me as an adult, assuming that the two of us were the intellectuals of the family. Uncle was an avid reader and perhaps that also contributed to the instability of his career; for if he was deep in a book, he did not bother to mend the watches or repair the bracelets piling up on his bench. And, if the man at the second-hand book store had a volume he desired, Uncle was quite capable of trading a solid gold brooch or a valuable pair of earrings for it, if cash happened to be short.

I loved books too, and he saw in me a kindred spirit—at least he made me think he did. I still have books that he gave me, *The Intellectual Life* and *A Village of Vagabonds*. Somehow I think that the titles are significant. What he enjoyed he liked to share, and, dear as Hetty was to him, she did not have the intellectual turn of mind that complimented his. He was fond of writing letters, and, when he was not with us, he wrote long letters to my aunt and to me, giving, in an angular and spidery hand, his views on life and philosophy and politics and books. I have one letter in which he tells in meticulous detail for several pages just how Boston baked beans should be properly prepared, and how as a boy on Sunday mornings he had been sent out to the baker's to purchase a pot of beans hot from the oven. Before the letter was over I could smell the beans and savor them on my tongue—it was all so very vivid.

Uncle Ash was a truly self-educated man, for he had been obliged to leave school when he was twelve in order to provide for his mother and younger brothers and sisters. Perhaps the most truly educated persons are those who educate themselves. There is never a time when they say, "Now I have graduated, my education is finished." The man who does not graduate but who yearns for learning says, "I cannot rest here, the others are so far ahead of me." So perhaps he passes all of them and never even knows it.

Uncle Ash's father was a New England sea captain in the days of sailing ships, and he was lost at sea. A jeweler took young Ashmun as an apprentice after his father disappeared and thus he learned the trade of mending watches, engraving, working in gold and silver that he practiced all his life. At one time, as a young man, he went out to the gold rush in Montana, hoping to do more with gold than use it to make settings for other people's jewels. I have a little filigree brooch on which he fixed a fairly sizable gold nugget, the only one of any consequence that his hopeful digging and panning produced. How characteristic of him that he did not turn it into money, but mounted it on a brooch and gave it away.

Grandma told me that when he was quite young he had lost his first wife in childbed fever, and the baby had died too. It was a long time later that he met Aunt Et when both of them were lonely.

When Aunty and Uncle came to visit there were great conversations. I sat entranced to hear them talking and remembering the times when they were young. Grandma and Aunt Et especially loved to go back into the past to talk about their childhood. It had been such a happy time, a time never quite equalled for either of them by the realities of their later lives. They spoke of their mother and father, called all the brothers and sisters by name, even the dogs and the horses. And there were so many stories and half-forgotten jokes that made them chuckle with delight. You would think that there had never been a family like the Woodhouse family—never a father so wise and kind, never a mother so quick-tempered but lovable, never children so full of pranks and jollity and happiness.

And all of the terrors and hopes and gratifications of pioneer life on the Wisconsin frontier came alive as they talked. I knew so much of it already, because, when I could not sleep, I crept in bed with Gram, begged her to tell a story, and she gladly went back to her childhood and shared it with me.

When Aunt Et was there the same stories came out again. They laughed and added details that were new to me and sometimes a whole new story that Gram had half forgotten. It was something wonderful to hear them. But often Uncle Ash would get fed up with stories of the Woodhouse family. He would jump out of his chair and stretch and say, "Oh, those Woodhouses! There never were a bunch of saints on God's green earth to compare with those Woodhouses!" He took Aunt Elsie and me into his rebellion against the Woodhouses as we mocked with him and pretended to be on his side, but yet we secretly envied and admired the solidarity of a family that never forgot a member and recalled home ties with such an enduring affection.

In the periods when they were happily settled and thriving, we sometimes went to visit "Sister Et and Brother Ash." There was always something special about the places where they lived. In Pasco there was an arbor hung with delicious grapes and Aunty made a thick, sweet, grape conserve with nuts in it. I still remember how marvelous this was on hot buttered toast. I think it was at Kennewick that there were apples, and Aunt made prodigious apple butter. Their gardens were always full of fresh peas, corn, and strange things like melons and oddly shaped, colored gourds.

But the happiest time I ever had with them was on Whidbey Island in Puget Sound. I had been ill during the summer and the doctor had recommended a warmer climate for the winter. Aunt Elsie and I were on our way to California, but first we were going to take "Sister Caddie" to Whidbey Island to spend the winter with Etta and Ash. From Everett, Washington, we took a little ferry boat that landed us on Whidbey Island. Just outside the tiny town of Langley, Uncle and Aunty had a farm where they raised dewberries and celery for the market, along with all sorts of vegetables for themselves.

Down at the corner of the farm, where their private road touched the common road to Langley, Uncle had a tiny jewelry shop. There the watches to be mended hung above the bench and a small show-case held wedding and engagement rings and inexpensive baubles for Christmas or birthday or graduation presents. I see Uncle sitting there at his bench with the mysterious jeweler's loupe fixed in his eye, his moustache bristling, the sparse hairs on top of his head in disarray, and his clever fingers busy repairing or engraving or resetting some inexpensive jewel. The trade from Langley was not brisk, but the farm gave them substance.

They lived in the largest and most pleasant house that I remember. It sat on a hill above the dewberry bushes and the celery trenches; Aunty had furnished and arranged it charmingly. They had a horse, a cow, some sheep, and pigs. Except for sugar and salt and flour they were almost self-sufficient.

I must have been eleven at the time because I still played with dolls. I had brought several of the dearest ones with me to keep me company in far-off California. Aunt Elsie and I were to stay a week before we started south. It was autumn with chill fogs and vapors drifting in from the surrounding sea. I remember it as a gray time, snug indoors with Aunty's superb cooking, and rigorous but not too cold outside.

Uncle took time off from shop and farm to give me a happy experience. We went to the beach and collected the little plaid limpet shells, the smooth and pretty pebbles, the odd-shaped pieces of driftwood. I was an inland child and to me this was a great adventure. We went into the forest that edged the farm and dug the root of the licorice fern that could be chewed when it was dried. I had seen sticks of it before in glass jars at the drug store—but to dig it and dry it myself!

I do not remember who had the idea, but it was decided to give my dolls an early Christmas party. Aunty and I made tiny Christmas presents, little purses and books and pictures in tiny frames; Aunt Et's clever fingers crocheted miniature hats and sweaters. Then Uncle took me with him to the swamp at the edge of the forest, where we selected a very tiny, perfect Christmas tree exactly scaled to dolls. When it was set up on a box we trimmed it with popcorn and cranberries and bits of tinsel and colored paper. Aunty cut a six-pointed star of folded silver paper for the top of the tree. Then I helped her make cookies and a pitcher full of dewberry juice lemonade.

The preparations are clearer in my mind than the party, but there was magic in all of it. It is a time I shall never forget: the gray days full of healthy outdoor exercise, with warmth and friendliness within. I sensed that Aunty was completely content. If they could just have kept the farm, the shop, the pretty house, the forest, and the sea! But in a few years they were gone again.

The last memories I have of Uncle Ash are painful, and I hate to set them down. I had been married a few years and I wanted my great aunt and uncle to meet my husband and my little boy. I wanted my husband and son to know the old couple who had meant so much to me. We had been visiting Aunt Elsie and my grandmother, and, on our way home, we would pass near the small Western town where Uncle and Aunt were living. It was arranged that we should spend a night with them.

I remember that they were living in a large, barn-like building, in a corner of which Uncle had his bench and carried on his business, such as it was. It seemed to be dwindling rapidly. With screens and a clever arrangement of furniture, Aunty had made the large and barren room into the familiar home. She had embellished it with her fancywork and her painted china, and out behind the building she had a charming slat house full of vines and potted plants and blooming things. People always gave Aunty slips, and under her gentle fingers these cast-off bits of plants achieved a luxuriant beauty.

My husband and I were struggling to get a start in life so we had no rich possessions but our love. However, Raymond did have a beautiful gold watch that had been presented to him by his parents on his twenty-first birthday. The watch was running perfectly and we were both proud of it. Uncle Ash admired it and said that he would like to clean it for my husband. It would take a few days and then he would send it on to us. The watch did not seem to need cleaning and neither of us wished to part with it. But Uncle Ash was determined to do this service for us, so we did not like to refuse an old man's kindness. We left the watch and returned to our home in the Midwest.

The watch did not come, and it did not come. We looked to the mails in vain, and Raymond was seriously handicapped without a time piece. I began to feel not only embarrassed but apprehensive. We wrote to ask about the watch and Uncle replied that in cleaning the delicate mechanism he had found a faulty part and that he had sent away for a replacement. It might take some time. The weeks went by. There was a very bad period when I wondered if we would ever see the watch again. Finally we wrote begging him to send the watch as it was and we would try to find a replacement for the part among our local watchmakers. There was another long silence. Months passed; and then at last the watch arrived, and with it a sizable bill for new parts and repairs. I was disillusioned and angry — my lovely Uncle Ash, so generous and intellectual, so gay and loving!

We paid the bill out of our small budget. "I have my watch back anyway!" my husband said.

It took me quite a little time to realize what silent desperation must have underlaid the whole affair. Soon after the watch was returned Aunty and Uncle made their last move to another strange town. I did not see them again.

19

Eddie

M Y AUNT ELSIE was an impressionable woman caught between the pruderies of Victoria and the freer thinking of the Edwardians. She had an unbridled tongue and was likely to say quite indiscreet things that shocked us all, but inside she was completely virginal and was horrified by license in other people. She married very late in life, but during the years when most girls were getting tied up she rejected a number of proposals and suffered several unfortunate love affairs. She could never bring herself to accept the proposals, and the suitors who got away without proposing were the ones she lingeringly yearned for afterwards.

I was somewhat jealous of her suitors and doubtless I behaved badly, but I was also a convenient excuse for her when she felt that the affair had progressed so far as to threaten her virginity. "You will have to take my darling little girl if you take me," she said. "My beloved sister left her in my care, and she and I can never be parted." At this point the tentative proposers usually ran the other way. I would have been happy alone with my grandmother, and I used to feel that Aunt Elsie took unfair advantage of our relationship by driving her young men away with threats of me. Why couldn't she have told them "no" without passing the guilt to me?

There was one occasion, however, when the kind young man seemed to be willing to be saddled with an orphan niece. He was a fair-haired, ruddy-cheeked young man named Eddie Offits, and he was sent to our town from a nearby city to help untangle some financial affairs at one of our banks. He was to be in our town for six weeks. I'm not sure how my aunt met him, but her voluble tongue and dominant personality ensnared him before his six weeks were half over.

"You remind me of my mother," he said. "I miss her when I have to be away from home, and you have made me feel so welcomed. I haven't had a lonely moment since I met you."

Aunt was pleased and flattered. At last we thought that she was seriously contemplating matrimony.

"Oh, Eddie," she said, "I do love you. We can be so happy together."

Gram looked at Eddie with her searching eyes that broke his physiognomy down into tell-tale bumps and creases, but she said nothing. She would have been glad to see her daughter married to a safe and suitable man, and Eddie seemed not only suitable but safe.

After banking hours, when Eddie had eaten dinner at the hotel, he walked up the hill and sat on our front porch behind the screen of Thousand Beauty climbing roses and held Aunt's hand. Grandma and I busied ourselves with the dishes, or we sat under the light at the dining room table. I read or drew pictures while Gram looked at the newspaper again or mended clocks or broken harnesses. Ordinarily she would have enjoyed sitting on the porch in the summer dark, smelling the roses, her hands clasped idly on her ample stomach. But we respected the rules of courtship and left the youngish couple alone in the romantic light from the corner arc lamp that sifted through a network of leaves and branches to dapple the porch swing.

As we worked at our indoor occupations we could hear Aunt's voice going lickety-split in her usual sprightly comment on the world, and Eddie's gentle monosyllable occasionally punctuating the brief pauses. I thought to myself that lovers ought to be more silent, but then I was very inexperienced and Romeo and Juliet had certainly had a lot to say to each other even when they were in momentary danger of being discovered. So perhaps it was all right.

Eddie gave Aunt an engagement ring, quite a nice little diamond set in solid gold. We all admired how it flashed in the sun and threw colored sparks of light on the wall as she turned her hand back and forth. They did not set a date, although Grandma could not see why they needed to wait. After all, they were both well into the age of discretion.

"Well," Aunt said, "Eddie wants me to meet his mother first, and, of course, I want to do so. She must be a very dear little old lady from all that he has told me; and she may have to live with us some day, if Eddie's older brother ever gets married again."

"Maybe she would go to live with the older brother," Grandma suggested.

"Oh, no," Aunt said, "at least Eddie thinks not. Eddie is the baby of the family, you see. His mother raised three children alone. It seems the father ran away and left them when they were little or something dreadful of that kind, and she had to rear them all by herself."

"Well, dear, I hope you'll be happy," Grandma said.

"Oh, I shall! I shall!" cried Aunt with cheerful vehemence.

It was settled that after Eddie returned to Spokane my aunt would go for a week's visit and then the engagement would be formally announced. Aunt sewed and mended and washed and ironed, and, when she left, with her satchel neatly packed, she looked very nice indeed.

"Don't talk too much, dear," Gram said.

"Oh, I won't," said Aunt.

I was terribly lonesome after she was gone.

"You'll have to get used to it," Grandma said. "This is for a week. It'll be for all time when she gets married."

"But she's going to take me with her when she gets married. She made Eddie promise."

"Would you want to go?"

"No, not really," I said. "I'd rather stay with you."

"Eddie's mother would be there," said Grandma. "You'd have another dear old lady for a grandma."

"Oh, Gram," I cried in sincerest love and praise, "*you*'re not a dear old lady."

Several days dragged by and it really was lonesome without Aunt. Her busy chatter usually filled the house, and she was full of cheerful projects for cutting paper lace doilies, or making pictorial plaques by pouring wet plaster of Paris into saucers that contained photographs, or manufacturing beads by rolling glued triangles of colored paper around hatpins. Gram was the central axis about whom I revolved, but Aunt was my chief source of entertainment.

"How many more days until she comes back?" I wondered.

"Look at the kitchen clock," Grandma said. The kitchen clock was the wonder of my youth, and it was Grandma's pride. It had been in Grandpa's office, and, after his death, she had not been able to give it up. This was not so much for sentimental reasons; she just knew that she was the only one who could keep it in proper running order. It had a very large face which not only told the time to the second, but also the day of the week and the month. It had a small glass-encased pendulum that winked as it wagged back and forth. It hung on the kitchen wall near the back door.

According to the calendar on the kitchen clock, Aunt would be back in three more days.

But we had scarcely finished consulting the clock when there was a noise at the front door. Someone was coming in without ringing the bell. We both ran to see, but I was nimbler than Grandma.

I threw myself into Aunt's arms. "Oh, Aunt! Aunt! We've missed you terribly!"

She gently disengaged my clinging arms, took off her hat, and laid it on the table. She looked somewhat more rumpled and crushed than she had looked when she left us, and for a few moments she was unnaturally silent.

"Well, daughter," Grandma said, "we didn't expect you home quite so soon."

"Where is your lovely engagement ring, Aunt?" I asked.

"Sit down and I'll tell you," she said.

"Do you want anything? There's still coffee on the back of the stove."

"I could use some coffee. I caught the early train. I didn't have any breakfast."

"Oh, Aunt, what happened?"

"They had a lovely house," Aunt said, between sips of coffee and bites of Gram's good homemade bread. "It smelled of floor wax and there were stained glass fans over the windows, and Eddie was so proud of me and everything was very nice."

"Yes?" Grandma prompted.

Aunt spread some homegrown, homemade plum jam on the thick slice of bread and took a thoughtful bite.

"It was a lovely place, up a steep flight of cement steps, with a knocker on the door, and there was a garden out back with better roses than we have. I liked his brother too. He was quite bald but otherwise very handsome. He called me 'sister'—imagine that!"

"Yes? Yes?" said Grandma.

"Well, Mrs. Offits was very large and imposing, really a very handsome woman. I can't think why Eddie was always saying I reminded him of her, because I don't think I. . . . Am I at all imposing or impressive? I never thought so. And she approved of me — she really did. She said, 'You are just right for Eddie, dear. I have always known that some day I must give him up, but I feared it might be to some silly little blonde who would have to be taken care of. He needs the care and attention that I know you can give him. You look so sensible.' Yes, she said that, and she was very careful never to leave us alone together. Oh, she was quite proper, not at all as I had imagined her."

"Not a dear little old lady?" I inquired.

"Not quite as I imagined," said Aunt, "but very forceful. Eddie seemed much younger there than here, and he is such a dutiful son, and everything was really lovely, the roast beef was done to perfection, and he has a married sister who lives just around the corner. Mrs. Offits had picked out a house for Eddie and me that was just around the corner too. We were going to look at it tomorrow. She picks out his ties and socks too. She said, 'I hope you'll always let me do that for my baby. I know his tastes so well.' I said, 'Yes, Mother Offits'. She liked to have me call her that. Somehow all of us seemed to do what she liked to have us do. Only Arthur, he is Eddie's brother, said something odd to me. He said, 'So you're going to let her suck you in along with the rest of us?' Well, that made me a little uneasy. Arthur had been married, it seems, and lived just around the corner, but his wife ran off and left him and now he's living at home again. He's in the bank, too. They're all quite successful. 'Mother brought us up to be successful,' Eddie said. 'You won't realize what a wonderful woman she is until you have known her for a while.'

"You never saw such dahlias as they have, and an enlarged photograph of Eddie's mother over the parlor mantel, tinted in natural colors and a gilded frame. They have two kinds of hot cereal and bacon and eggs for breakfast. 'I have to feed my growing boys,' Mrs. Offits said. Oh, it was very nice."

"But you didn't have any breakfast before you took the train this morning, Elsie," Grandma said.

"No, I got up very early and walked to the station," Aunt said. "I left a note on the pin cushion."

"But why? If it was all so nice?"

"Well, I'll tell you," Aunt said. "Last night, when Mrs. Offits was seeing me to bed — she always left Eddie downstairs reading the paper when she took me to my room and kissed me goodnight, just like a mother."

"Not like me," said Grandma dryly.

"Well, I mean, just like a suitor's mother, I suppose," said Aunt. "Well, just before she left me at the door of the guest room (such a pretty room, the guest room!) she said, 'Oh, while I think of it, just let me show you how I make up Eddie's bed. You'll have to know before you are married, of course.'

"So I followed her down the hall to Eddie's room. There were a lot of pennants over Eddie's bed, although I don't believe he ever went away to college, and a row of Horatio Alger books on a shelf near the window. But what Mrs. Offits wanted to show me was the foot of the bed. She lifted up the mattress and she said, 'You see, I pin his blankets down with safety pins. He's always been a restless sleeper, and this is the only way I can be sure that his feet are covered in the night. I knew that you'd want to do the same for my darling baby boy.'

"Well," Aunt said, "I thought it all over last night and I knew if I hurried this morning I could catch the early train home. It would be easier that way than telling them all goodbye, and I left the engagement ring folded into the thank-you note that I fastened to the pin cushion."

"Oh, Aunt," I said, "we're glad to have you back."

"Yes, and do you know what?" Aunt said.

"No. What?"

"Eddie's sister makes beads out of mashed-up rose leaves. They still keep the scent of the roses. You and I will have to start saving up rose leaves. What do you think?"

"Oh, goody!" I said. We were back to normal.

20

The Edgetts

As I was growing up I was called periodically on the telephone by a woman who was nearer the age of my grandmother than of me. I never knew what to say to her, and I stood uncomfortably beside the wall telephone that was a little too high for me, answering her questions and listening with impatience to her long harangues.

"Yes, I like school. No, I'm in the seventh grade now. Yes, I'm doing well. Yes, Grandma is well. No, I didn't go to the Sunday school picnic. No, I didn't notice. Did it rain yesterday? You heard it on the roof? Oh, yes, of course."

I knew that Mrs. Edgett was sitting comfortably at a telephone the right height for her, and, in my mind's eye, I could see her: her head cocked at a listening angle; her sightless eyes fixed on the distant wall; her large, shapeless body spilling over the sides of her chair. I answered as politely as I could because I understood that the telephone was her one diversion. She called all sorts of people. She called my grandmother and my aunt, and, when she had exhausted far more rewarding conversationalists than myself, she called me.

The Edgetts had come to town in the very early days when my grandmother and grandfather came from Missouri. The two families had known each other back there, but the ties had never been very close ones. The Edgetts had a little house on the side of the hill below us. The house hung on the hillside precariously with stilts on the lower side to keep it from falling into the ravine, and the old board sidewalk that went down the hill beside it had cleats to keep pedestrians from slipping. Horses and carriages went around by Third Street instead of risking the hill, and, although the Edgett hill was a short cut to town for us, we went around by Third Street as well.

I don't know when nor why Mrs. Edgett went blind. We accepted the fact as naturally as we accepted the fact that the dogs of town hated the postman. It was one of those things. Yet I always remember her listening face, the face of a person vitally interested in the world and curious about people, but only able to get impressions through her ears and her touch.

The women of town dreaded to hear the phone ring. In the midst of making jelly or writing a letter or baking an apple pie, she would say, "This is Mrs. Edgett. How are you, dear?" and simple courtesy kept them standing on aching feet, knowing that the jelly was bubbling over or the pie getting too brown while the seemingly endless conversation went on. In those days the telephone was for ordering groceries or delivering brief messages of life or death. I believe that Mrs. Edgett was the first person to use the telephone for purely social purposes.

There was always something dreadfully wrong with the Edgetts. The mother went blind, the father died, the eldest son and daughter married unsuitably and never made a success of life, the youngest son was mentally retarded. They were all ponderously overweight and they breathed heavily when they talked and were short of breath when they climbed their hill. But they had one shining asset, Ruthie, the middle daughter.

Ruthie was grossly overweight as they all were, and she was not particularly pretty. She was a year or two older than I was, I suppose, and we knew each other casually in church and in school. I remember hearing a girl with a harelip, who was not very personable herself, saying with scorn of Ruthie Edgett, "The's dust a big, fat thlob, Ruthie is — a big, fat thlob!" It is impossible to reproduce on paper the odd enunciation of the girl with the harelip, but it was a gruesome example of the pot calling the kettle black, and Ruthie Edgett deserved better treatment, for she was bright and willing and strong enough to bear the burdens of her faltering family on her broad shoulders.

When the rest of us were scattering rose petals through high school, Ruthie relinquished the pursuit of learning and went to work in a department store. How else would the family be clothed and fed? For all her weight she was very light on her feet and she moved briskly about her work, pleasing customers with her alacrity and understanding. She did most of the housework before and after store hours, and she kept her mother clean and able to find her way to the telephone.

Mrs. Edgett learned certain skills that helped her to pass the long hours while Ruthie was at the store. It was said that she could bake bread and that she could tell when it was done by the sound it made when she tapped it with her thimble. But she had become blind late in life and there was no one in town with the knowledge to teach her how to compensate for her loss. There were no talking books, no radio, but God had sent her the telephone.

I often think of Ruthie Edgett and how brave she was, how cheerful, how willing, how kind to everyone. So far as I know she never had a boyfriend, but perhaps she was too busy to notice. She was always hurrying to do her duty to someone and smiling as she bustled.

Sometimes, even yet, when I am busy and the telephone rings, I have a sharp presentiment that it will be Mrs. Edgett. "Yes, thank you, I am fine. Yes, Grandma is fine too. No, I'm in the seventh grade this year. Yes, the sun is shining today. Didn't you know? But, of course, how could you . . . ?"

21

My Townspeople on
the Fourth of July

THE FOURTH OF JULY has shrunk in size since I was a child. It used to be the biggest day of the year. Easter was something we celebrated solemnly in church; Christmas was hard candy and small presents in stockings and sometimes a tree perilously lighted with flaming candles. But for all its charm, Christmas was an indoor event, good for large families, but often a trifle bleak for Grandma and Aunt and me in a house alone with drifts of snow outside.

The Fourth of July was sunshine and noise and company; it was bliss and danger and sentiments that lifted and tossed the heart. Perhaps we were more patriotic than religious in those days. Today our holidays seem to lack both patriotism and religion. They have become extra bits of leisure in the oceans of leisure that have been provided for us by electricity and a paternal government, a government that no longer seems to belong to us personally as it did in the early 1900s.

In my childhood we prepared for the Fourth of July for weeks in advance. Sunday school choirs rehearsed patriotic anthems; we worked and saved our money for fireworks. How we laid out our money on fireworks was terribly important. If we spent a dollar recklessly our whole fortune might go skyward in two minutes or fizzle out in even less time.

Grandma used to say, "Don't squander all your money on a couple of skyrockets. Think. Think. Get your money's worth." So I learned thrift at the same time that I was spending good money on ephemerality that would soon go up in smoke.

The choice was dazzling. We used to stand before the fireworks counter in a blissful agony of indecision. There were clusters of tiny Chinese firecrackers that would all go off in one string, pop! pop!

pop! pop! There were firecrackers of every size up to the giant crackers that were tall and red and reminded me of the standpipe on the hill that provided our local water supply. There were sparklers and torpedoes and snakes, flowerpots and grasshoppers, volcanos and Red Devils. There were pinwheels, large and small, and Roman candles. Ah, the perilous delight of holding a Roman candle well out from the body and waving it gently back and forth in a large semi-circle while it spluttered bright sparks, periodically emitting balls of colored fire! Each time a colored ball hissed out, a tremor shook the arm that held the candle. The darkness palpitated with colored balls.

Finally there were the expensive and magnificent sky rockets. We could only afford a few of those and Grandma built us a special trough, tilted up at the correct angle to guide them on their way. Grandma adored fireworks. Perhaps that is why the July Fourths on our hill were so very memorable. I sometimes think how Grandma would have enjoyed the pyrotechnics at Cape Kennedy. Yet again, perhaps not. She would have wanted to set them off herself.

Before the first rooster crowed the first firecracker went off in our town on the Fourth of July. We children had been sleeping with ears cocked, and now we arose as one child, pulling on our clothes. Shivering in the summer dawn, we rushed out to explode our first firecrackers. Suddenly the town was crackling and popping from end to end. Only the dogs were unhappy. Our Rowdy ran under Grandma's bed, lying there shivering and shaking all day long. For him it was Armageddon, the Day of Judgment. He never could remember that he had lived through it the year before. Sometimes I tried to pull him out from under the bed and reason with him, but he only stared at me with strange, suffering eyes that glowed in the darkness and did not recognize me. This was the only flaw in my otherwise perfect day.

Our best Fourth was the one when the two girls next door and I pitched a tent in the side yard. In front of it we had dug what we called a "furnace." This was a hole in the ground covered by a large flattened tin can with a piece of stovepipe at the back. In it we built fires and cooked delectable breakfasts of bacon and eggs and burned toast. Breakfast was wonderful, but we could not linger over it,

because we were riding in the parade at ten o'clock. My Iceland pony
and two-wheeled cart were always in demand for the parade. We
had the only Iceland pony in town, so we went all out to decorate
the cart with flags and paper flowers and bunting. We gave the pony
patriotic cockades and wound the cart wheels with red, white, and
blue bunting. In our best white dresses we felt superb.

Aunt and the mothers of the other girls saw us off with pride.
Then they put on their best hats and walked down to Main Street
to see us ride by, in line with the five business floats, the high school
band, the Civil War veterans, the decorated horseback riders and
bicyclists, the buggies full of politicians and speakers of the day, the
Latah County Pioneers, the Eagles and the Woodmen of the World,
the Ladies' Auxiliary of the G. A. R. and the girls' chorus. I have
never forgotten the heady exhilaration of riding in a parade.

The parade broke up at the city park, and there the patriotic
speeches began. I took the pony home, unhitched him, and gave
him some oats. Then I hurried back to the park in time to sing "Tent-
ing Tonight," "The Battle Hymn of the Republic," and "The Star-
Spangled Banner" along with the girls' chorus.

Time was taken out for lunch between the morning and the afternoon program of speeches. Here the mothers shone. Hampers
and bags of food appeared; everything was set out on long tables
made of planks laid across trestles. Cold fried chicken, deviled eggs
and potato salad, lemonade and chocolate cake – our appetites were
splendid. I particularly remember some of the delicacies that I never
see anymore: the tiny, cold, baking-powder biscuits filled with deviled ham; the wonderful six-layer strawberry shortcakes, made the
day before and chilled, that were cut into wedge-shaped slices, served
up like ordinary cake. And the watermelons, oh, the watermelons!

The afternoon speeches were somewhat lost on us children who
had been up since dawn. We played tag on the edges of the crowd
or curled up in the shade and went to sleep. But consciously or un-
consciously we absorbed a lot of spread-eagle patriotism.

Itching with sunburn and aching with fatigue, we dragged ourselves home before sunset. It had been a hot day and we were glad
to kick off our shoes and socks and gather our forces for the evening. We counted our fireworks over again to be sure that nothing

was missing. The crackers had been used up in the early morning, but the loveliest pieces were still to come.

Grandma never went to the parade or the celebration in the park. She had a bad heart; she saved herself for the evening. So now she gave us a supper of homemade bread and milk in the cellarway where the cool air, laden with a mysterious apple-y, cheese-y smell, came up from below to soothe our spirits.

When it was dark and very much cooler we went out to the hitching block in front of our gate to light our punks. The punks had a smell like incense and they added to the faintly oriental flavor that had permeated our very American day. For, after all, how could we have been so wonderfully American without the ingenuity of the Chinese?

Our house was at the top of a hill, and also at the dead end of a short street that led steeply downward in front. We could see the other people's fireworks all over town, and they could see ours. Our hill was a natural place for the neighborhood children to gather.

Now Grandma was in her element. Even the fathers of the other children let her run the show. Her bad heart was forgotten as she took command. We had order and dignity in our procedure. Yet every child had the independent pleasure of firing his own purchases. Grandma never took anything out of any child's hand, but she would not tolerate wild and indiscriminate shooting off in all directions. We started with the smaller pieces and worked toward the massive ones. Everybody's contribution was given its time and place and its proper chorus of "oh's" and "ah's." How bright the stars were in the dark sky overhead, and how our own stars put them out with brighter golds and reds and crimsons! Oh, lovely night of star and stripes, I shall never forget you!

Of course, that was the night that Billie Sweeney had his fingers so badly burned because he held the giant cracker too long before he threw it. That happened across town, not on Grandma's hill, and Grandma said it just went to show how careful we should be.

But there were no deaths on the highway.

22

Governor McConnell and
Professor Collins

THE LATAH COUNTY Historical Society has made a museum of the old McConnell mansion. The house was given to the county by its last owner, Dr. Frederic C. Church, who, until his death in 1966, was professor of history at the University of Idaho. I never knew Dr. Church, although I understand that he is as worthy of a personal memoir as any of the other mansion inhabitants. I have many random memories of the old house, and perhaps they are worth setting down.

I remember once, when I was quite small, that I saw the original owner and builder of the house walking down Third Street, and someone said to me, "There goes Governor McConnell. Remember that you have seen him."

He was always Governor McConnell to the people of our town, although he was ex-governor to all of the other people of the state. As a child I believed that he was the first governor of Idaho, but I am told now that he was the second or third.[10] At any rate for us he was *the* Governor. I own a copy of his *Early History of Idaho,* which is a curiously unscientific mixture of fascinating anecdote and day-by-day recording of purely routine matters—"unassimilated," perhaps that is the word for it. He was a man of action rather than a social scientist. As well as being governor he was one of Idaho's first senators, and, what was perhaps an equally great distinction, he was the father-in-law of Senator William E. Borah. The mental picture that I retain of Governor McConnell is that of a small, stocky man in a dark suit with flowing white hair and beard—a fleeting glimpse, then gone.

In 1883 he began to build a large American-Gothic house on one of our hills. It was finished in 1886 and is supposed to have cost, together with the furnishings, about $60,000, a large amount of money for those days.[11] It has been durable. So it stands there today, dignified, stiff, slightly formidable. I knew quite well the Adair girls who lived there during most of my childhood, but, except for a very vague recollection of some sort of formal birthday party, my memories of the house are not connected with children's play.[12] It was the type of house in which children did not play, it seems to me. Perhaps someone can contradict me on this. To me it always appeared sinister.

For many years after the governor's day, the mansion was a superior type of high-class rooming house. Only very select people, mostly university professors, were taken as roomers, and it was considered a distinct privilege to be able to stay at the McConnell mansion. On the second floor there was a large room (with connecting bedroom and bath, I believe) which was particularly desirable. It was the home for many years of an eccentric bachelor named Isaac Cogswell. Dr. Cogswell was head of the music department at the university and arbiter of musical taste for the whole community. Whenever there was a concert of any degree of importance he was there playing "Marche Militaire" with great intensity and virtuosity. I never heard him play any other piece, and this one still rings in my mind's ear just as he played it, his near-sighted eyes close to the piano, his powerful hands banging away with eloquent precision. He must have loved "Marche Militaire" very much to have played it so often and so passionately. That it might have been the only concert piece in his repertoire was naturally unthinkable.

As a pupil of his I came to know the large room on the second floor of the governor's mansion with horrendous intimacy. The grand piano, the partly shuttered windows, the long and slippery staircase to the upper regions, the bleakness of it all comes back to me now with overwhelming oppression.

I enjoy music when somebody else makes it, but I am not a music maker. In fact, I have a mental block about music-making that would give psychoanalysts a field day to explain. I understand the mental block pretty well myself. I had a beautiful mother who was a gifted musician. She died young. My early youth was plagued by people who looked at her shy and awkward child, a child who resembled the father, and said to me, "What a beautiful and talented mother you had, dear. You are not a bit like her, are you? But perhaps you inherited her musical ability? Do you play the piano, dear?" The answer was "no," and "no, no, no!"

But my failure to perform was not because of lack of interest on the part of my family. "Her mother was a lovely musician," reasoned my aunt, "therefore we must make one of her too." Even Dr. Cogswell, the supreme commander, who had known my mother and sometimes played duets with her, even he agreed to see what he could do with me, although it was not his habit to bother with untalented children.

So I trudged drearily up the long slippery staircase, conscious that, when I sat down at the grand piano, absolutely nothing would come out, that "The Good Fairy Waltz" was beyond me, that my fingers could not follow the intricacies of "Sweet Clover," nor could my mind untangle the 4-4 beat of "Little Toy Soldier on Parade." I knew and marvelled at how dumb I was. In other fields of endeavor I had a healthy respect for my capabilities, but here I was defeated before I began. No one knows how I suffered.

Dr. Cogswell didn't. He welcomed me every week with some measure of gradually ebbing hope in the pale eyes behind the thick lenses. For my mother's sake he gave me the benefit of the doubt. I was grateful to him, but, at the same time, I understood that there must come a snapping point for anybody's patience. I used to sit down at the piano with actual fear that some day he would take me by the heels and dash my brains out against the wall in a fit of rage at my incredible stupidity. Actually, I suppose, I had nothing to fear from him. But I still shudder at the thought of a grand piano in a partially shuttered room at the head of a long slippery staircase.

Yet, later that room was to become a delightful place to me. If I did not know that it was the same room, my fancy would certainly deceive me. What happened to Dr. Cogswell, I do not remember, but I assume that death removed him.

At the time that I became a freshman in college, the large room at the head of the stairs in the old McConnell house was inhabited by Professor Wilkie Collins of the English department. I can only suppose that Professor Collins had a romantic and literary-minded mother, who, when she married a Collins, determined at once that she would name her first born Wilkie. I never heard that he was in any other way connected with the Victorian novelist. The original Wilkie Collins, from all accounts, seems to have been a dull and uninteresting fellow, in spite of his lively imaginings concerning moonstones and women in white.

But *our* Wilkie Collins was an expansive, good-looking man with a rolling nautical gait that was supposed to have originated in his years of deck pacing in the merchant marines. He had more of an affinity with Conrad than with the original Wilkie, and we all felt that he had *seen* life, not just read about it. This glamorous aura of having lived genuinely rather than vicariously is much more important to the freshman student than the authorities ever realize. We hung on Wilkie's every word, uttered in a lazy drawl that seemed to roll with the sea as surely as his walk did. He had a sense of humor that crinkled his round, deep-set eyes, turned up the corners of his ample mouth, and let us glimpse the white teeth in the well-tanned face. An English teacher, oh, assuredly more than that — an influence, certainly an influence!

We all competed for his casual favor. I remember how thrilled I was when he suggested that I might do some screening of pessimistic poetry for him in anticipation of a treatise on that subject that he proposed some day to write. I was at that stage of development when the pessimistic poets greatly appealed to me, and I leapt to the assignment with almost fanatical zeal. Actually I think that my enthusiasm frightened Professor Collins just a little bit. He had me into his office one day to ask if my health was good. He did not wish to run the risk of sending me into a psychic decline along with the pessimistic poets. But I must have convinced him of my physical soundness, for he let me continue with the project until my own interest gradually declined. I don't know what ever became of the treatise on pessimistic poetry. I have never heard of its being published, but then World War I came along and Wilkie Collins was one of the first to leave us to return to the merchant marine. Yes, he, like Governor McConnell, was a doer, not a commentator; but of course the war was another story, the end of a small and safe world that was still unchallenged for us when Wilkie lived on the second floor of the mansion.

Sometimes when I cannot sleep at night I put myself into a drowsy mood by repeating to myself Wordsworth's sonnet:

The world is too much with us; late and soon,
Getting and spending, we lay waste our powers;
Little we see in Nature that is ours;
We have given our hearts away, a sordid boon!

It usually works as a gentle soporific, and I am grateful for it. To learn this poem was one of the few rote requirements that Wilkie asked of his freshmen. In the main he was satisfied to give us large ideas and general concepts, not bothering with sterile specifics. But on this one point he was adamant. Every freshman had to be able to recite "The World Is Too Much with Us." It was like the church expecting every Christian to know the Lord's Prayer and the Twenty-third Psalm. Wilkie felt that every civilized teenager must have Wordsworth's sonnet on the tip of his tongue. Many of the boys in the class, while admiring Wilkie for his adventurous past, did not feel it essential to be civilized to this extreme extent. But Wilkie took valuable class time to make every student recite the poem until he was sure that each one had it. I remember still how some of the boys in vengeful frustration bellowed out the "Great God, I'd rather be a Pagan" line. But Wilkie only smiled his Mona Lisa smile and never gave up.

I have always hated to learn by rote, and consequently my stock of quotations is pitifully small. A few Walter de la Mare poems learned for fun in spite of myself, some totally useless lines from *Evangeline* knocked into me by a less perceptive teacher than Wilkie Collins, these and a very few others are among the paucity of poems that I can repeat word for word to myself in the dark hours of the night. But there is always the great, calming organ swell of "The World Is Too Much with Us" to fall back upon. I wonder how many other freshmen of the year 1914 in Idaho accompany their wakeful nights with the sonorous measures of a never-to-be-forgotten poem?

Wilkie Collins had no apparent female connections. He was so attractive that we all wondered at that and speculation ran wild. It was said that he had fled to the far west from a disastrous marriage. It was said that he was in love with a lady baritone. The fact was that nobody knew a thing, but the girls all loved him just as much as if they had known—maybe more.

It was a college custom for the various sororities to invite favorite professors to luncheon on Sunday noons, and Wilkie Collins was always in demand. The sororities tried to stagger their company luncheons somewhat, so that the same faculty members were not invited to several houses on the same day. Thus the Gamma Phi Betas might invite several admired professors to luncheon on the first Sunday of the month, while the Delta Gammas or Kappa Kappa Gammas might pick the second or the third Sundays for their entertaining. When company was not expected, the sorority sisters often came down to luncheon in curlers. I remember one such Sunday on which the Gamma Phis, unprepared for guests, were comfortably relaxed in old clothes, curlers, and bedroom slippers, when suddenly the doorbell rang and there stood Wilkie Collins, hungrily looking for lunch. No one knew what to do except to invite him in and give him pot luck. He did not seem to notice the curlers or the fact that there were no other guests beside himself. He had a fine flair for unaffected enjoyment; now he was content to be here and to make himself amusing. Instead of the company pot roast or stewed chicken with dumplings, he seemed to relish the lowly hash that the cook had prepared. His humorous invention flowed freely in anecdote and lazy comment. The girls forgot their curlers and bedroom slippers. It was a marvelous occasion. We talked about that luncheon for years, and it was made more memorable for us by the fact that the Delta Gammas, in their best clothes, had waited half an hour for a missing guest before they gave up and served the stewed chicken. Wilkie never knew the difference.

Toward the end of my freshman year I was invited to attend a select group of eight students who were to meet in Wilkie's rooms on alternate Sunday evenings. Two of my best friends, with whom I had collaborated on a prize-winning playlet, and another girl selected for her literary leaning were invited; there were four equally arty boys. The boys were mostly upper classmen while we girls were all freshmen. It was terribly flattering. To make matters more enticing, it was understood that the dean of women was seriously concerned; freshman girls meeting in a man's room with older boys! In those days it was an unthinkable situation, and perhaps we were riding the first faint ripple of the great tidal wave that was soon to sweep away all conventions and restrictions for the female undergraduate.

But actually nothing could have been more innocent or charming than those Sunday evenings in Wilkie's big room. We made toast on an old toaster and ate it with marmalade and tea. We were unabashedly ourselves, with life, death, love and the fabulous world to discuss and pronounce upon. After much cogitation we named ourselves the Sans Souci Club. This was shortened in private to the "Sans C Club," meaning "without chaperone." We read aloud things that we had written or had found admirable in the writings of published authors. Wilkie let us do the talking, but he invented informal little projects for us that seemed to be fun and not hard labor.

I remember that one of the boys and I were given the task of making a translation (which Wilkie said he very much needed) of a French libretto of *Le Jongleur de Notre Dame*. It was written in a complicated French verse form, and Wilkie never suggested what kind of translation we were to make. We decided to do one in the same rhyme and meter as the original French. We both knew French; we both wrote poetry; it would be very simple. We had a lot of fun. We spent hours at it with the concentration and alacrity that we seldom brought to school assignments. Miraculously we produced several pages of poetic translation. Then suddenly one day we found ourselves rhyming *"ditches"* with *"breeches."* We looked at each other and burst out laughing. After a few more feeble attempts we let the whole thing slide. Wilkie never rebuked us. I'm sure that he had achieved as much as he expected and he must have been more than satisfied.

Oh, the lovely Sans Souci Club! The war came and it was all over, but I remember it. I remember the light and gaiety and inspiration that filled the big room on the second floor of the old McConnell mansion. All of my memories of horror connected with the grand piano, the half-shuttered windows, the long, slippery staircase were overlaid with memories of warm and unalloyed pleasure. What wonders can be worked by a good teacher, a congenial subject, and the will to learn.

Some day I must visit the museum and see what the Latah County Historical Society has done with the big room at the top of the stairs. I hope that they have been kind to it.

23

Entertaining People

ENTERTAINMENT HAS GONE through many phases in my lifetime: stock companies; vaudeville; silent motion pictures; radio (the mysterious crystal sets that forward-looking boys of our acquaintance built); talking and then colored movies; then the final universal vulgarity and delight, T. V. What next? Who can imagine?

The stock companies that came to our small Western town must have been in the lowest bracket of talent and inspiration. But we loved them. Every Saturday afternoon we girls trooped down to the Bijou Theater to weep over *East Lynne* or roar over *Charlie's Aunt*. We were not always taken in by the aging ingenues, but we usually fell in love with the leading man. There was one in particular, a large, curly-haired blond, oozing masculinity. We adored him. I have forgotten his name, but I remember his Olympian splendor, his pure white soul, and chaste nobility. We were more inhibited than the girls who later swooned over Rudy Valee, the Beatles, and Elvis Presley, but we were just as badly smitten.

From my earliest days I had been taken to the theater. I was definitely under its spell. Yet I developed a slightly critical sense of proportion. When I went with my Aunt Win to see *Uncle Tom's Cabin,* I was brought home in disgrace. All of the girls had been weeping over the death of Little Eva. The curtain was lowered for an instant's glimpse of Greek columns and ads of Carson's Grocery, the Latah County bank, and Grice's Funeral Parlor; then it was raised again to reveal an empty stage except for a small table on which stood a statue of the Venus di Milo. To a chorus of weeping children, the Venus di Milo, symbol of Little Eva's soul, was slowly drawn up by a wire to heaven. I was the only one who laughed, and I was scolded all the way home.

"Well," Grandma said when Aunt Win complained of me, "she's just a little girl compared to you. You can't expect too much of her."

"But, Mama, I was *so* humiliated. All the other girls were crying!"

Entertainment is a mixture of laughing and crying; I expect I was as entertained as all the girls who wept. Probably I have remembered it longer because I had behaved scandalously. I also laughed hard the time when one of Ben Hur's horses got off the treadmill and stood placidly gazing around him while his five companions were galloping furiously against a moving backdrop.

The art theater of today with its cubes and planes and shafts of light does not in any way resemble the old theater of attempted realism. The racing chariots with real horses, the heroines strapped to railway tracks with real or almost-real trains hooting toward them, the fires of hell, and the waterfalls into which virgins threw themselves, all these have given place to the flat reality of photography. If the old illusions sound ridiculous today, at least they had three dimensions, and we were naive enough to delight in them.

We had the summer Chautauqua in large tents at the edge of the city park where I heard my first opera, *The Chimes of Normandy;* sometimes at the university we saw the Ben Geet players, but the big travelling stars never got beyond Spokane.

Aunt and I used to take the electric train to Spokane to see Forbes Robertson in *Hamlet* or *The Passing of the Third Floor Back,* and Maud Adams in *Peter Pan* or *The Little Minister,* and Otis Skinner in *Mr. Antonio* or *Kismet.* There was a real matinee idol, Otis Skinner! And *Kismet* a real illusion, a vision I have kept intact. The musical version never had the authenticity and glamour of the play with Otis Skinner doing Hadjii, the beggar.

When we went to Spokane we stayed at the Davenport Hotel and we always had French pastries and tamales — French pastries at the Davenport or the Silver Grill, and superb tamales at a little Mexican restaurant somewhere down the street. Entertainment wasn't only in the theater but in the whole adventure, and perhaps the best moment of all was when the fiddles started tuning in the orchestra pit before the curtain rose.

But there was one episode in my childhood when the theater almost lost one of its most devoted admirers. It was an episode connected with the curly-blond and stainless male who played the stock company leads. He was triumphant and unassailable in his roles. He was magnanimous and right. Did he live off stage? Did he eat and sleep and walk like other men? We could not imagine it.

But one day a friend and I saw him! It was broad daylight and he was walking on the streets of town. Our ecstasy at seeing our hero in this too, too solid flesh, honoring our town by walking abroad in it, was somewhat tempered by the fact that he was accompanied by a dowdy female and two small children. And they were quarreling. When they came to a curb, one of the little children had difficulty in negotiating it. Instead of stooping tenderly to help the baby up, our hero took his foot and kicked the child onto the next level. The four went on ahead of us, the children crying, the adults quarreling noisily as they went. Oh, Ben Hur's horses! Little Eva's soul! The theater was almost lost to me at that moment. But I have rallied. I have learned not to look beyond the asbestos curtain or the pale blue scrims in search of the real character of the actors. Let entertainment suffice. There is so little of it.

24

Belle and Chuck

"HONOR THY FATHER AND THY MOTHER" meant blind obedience as well as honor in the early 1900s. But even then youth sometimes rebelled, and we had several romantic elopements in our town. One of the girls from our insular aristocracy ran away with an ill-paid professor against the physical opposition of her parents, and two or three other strong-willed juniors flouted their parents' wishes to assert their own. But the most sensational elopement to me was that of my friend and contemporary Belle Williams. To understand Belle, one must go back to her mother.

Mrs. Williams was a small, handsome woman with very black hair and sparkling black eyes. She had a look of foreignness that the town immediately suspected, and she lived for clothes. That she was not accepted into society, such as we knew it, made no difference to her in choosing her clothes. She wore them on the street if she was not invited to the parties. I did not know anything of her background or why she had so few friends in town. Whether through disdain or proud timidity, she let us all alone and we let her alone.

Everyone liked her husband, a tall, easy-going man who only asserted himself in the drugstore that he ran with competence. At home — a neat house full of shiny surfaces and artificial flowers — people said that he let Mrs. Williams dominate him and that he never raised a word of dissent because of the temper tantrum that might crash about his ears.

Into this household where Mrs. Williams had reigned supreme for so long that no one expected it to grow larger, fate or the careless stork dropped a baby daughter. Mrs. Williams named the baby Belle, and everyone expected a replica of the mother, small, elegant and disdainful, dark as a gypsy and smartly turned out.

Now that Mrs. Williams had two people to dominate her horizon widened, but only a little bit. The baby, being a female and helpless, could be molded and ornamented as the mother wished. The sewing machine began to whir.

I first became aware of Belle at the children's parties I attended. These were principally birthday parties where we played games and ate too much richly frosted cake and heavy ice cream that had melted in the little paper cartons in which it was carried from the ice cream parlor. How many times have I gone home from a summer birthday party, sweating from "Run, Sheep, Run" and overloaded with melting strawberry ice cream and had to lie on the dining room couch with a cold cloth on my head and a slop jar conveniently placed on a newspaper nearby? In spite of these agonies, I never forgave my parents for allowing me to be born in December, a month of school and snow and Christmas and New Year's—no decent time for a child's birthday.

At the parties Belle was the very long-legged child with the very short French dresses. How Belle came into society and her mother did not, I never understood. But the parents who drew the line at Mrs. Williams were always willing to include Belle. Perhaps this was because of her father who was genuinely liked, or perhaps it had something to do with Belle herself. She had an unpretentious simplicity that did not evoke hostility.

Belle grew very tall and long-legged like her father. She lacked her mother's vivid coloring, and at an early age she began to wear glasses. Her small head on a long neck, small red mouth, gray eyes (magnified to large proportions by the lenses of her glasses) gave her an appearance of gentle vulnerability that surprised us all.

Mrs. Williams must have been shocked to see what she had brought forth, but she never gave up on Belle. When the rest of us wore white muslin dresses just below our knees, Belle wore ruffles and tucks and yards of lace insertion that struck her long legs between the knee and the upper thigh. When we wore blue serge dresses and brown wool coats with home-knit mufflers, Belle wore little scarlet coats trimmed in white rabbit fur or swans down. We liked her as well as any other girl. If her mother had let her alone, we might even have loved her.

What she thought of herself and her relationship to her mother and to the girls of town, we never knew. She kept her own counsel, but, remembering how I was often embarrassed by the good intentions of my aunt, I used to wonder if she did not suffer for the clothes she had to wear and for the differentness of the mother who ruled her. Children accept easily. Belle grew up among us, and we became accustomed to her. We ceased to marvel at the scarlet coats and fur collars, and later at the smart suits and hats that none of us could achieve for ourselves even if we had the money.

When we reached college age, even with a university in town, there was a splitting up of high school friendships and loyalties. Some of the boys went into business with their fathers or branched out for themselves; some of the girls married young or began to clerk in the stores. I doubt if either of Belle's parents had gone to college, but Belle was slated from the beginning for the academic life. She joined those of us who yearned for higher learning and the social whirl of sororities and fraternities.

"She'll have the best," her mother said — grimly, no doubt, for she must have realized by this time that she was working with difficult material. The girls in the sorority that I had recently joined said of Belle, "She wears such lovely clothes. We *must* have her."

"She's nice too," we town girls said. But no one listened to us. Her clothes were all that the out-of-town girls could see. They had not become accustomed to her clothes through long association as we had, and they were unable to see beyond them to her quiet virtues.

"Of course she'd be a scarecrow without the clothes," someone said, but everybody shushed her. Some of us knew better.

Boys scarcely look at clothes. They saw that Belle was too tall, was flat-chested and slightly round-shouldered, that she wore glasses and had very little to say, and, while they had no other objection to her, they were not in a hurry to ask her for dates. The upper classmen of the sorority did all they could for her by arranging dates for college dances, but Belle did not project herself, and after a while they grew tired of pushing her. "Well, let her sink or swim," they said.

Meanwhile Belle's mother was as much in control as ever. If a young man came to her house at the bidding of some upperclassman in his own fraternity, Mrs. Williams took over where Belle faltered. She fed him, she flattered him, she put on her most elegant attire for him, and she did the talking for Belle. Most of the young men ran away in alarm.

"Why doesn't Belle stand up for herself?" we grumbled, but that was a habit that Belle had never acquired.

Once Belle had a sorority party at her house. Nothing could subdue a group of twenty girls and even Mrs. Williams, in her spotlessly elegant decor with the artificial flowers in the shiny vases and the embroidered Spanish shawl on the grand piano, did not keep us from shouting and laughing. But I saw Mrs. Williams standing in the background and looking at us with her bright black eyes, and I knew that Belle would not be allowed to invite us again.

Then toward the end of Belle's senior year something surprising happened. A good-looking, blond young man, who had always been popular with the sorority girls, invited Belle to his fraternity dance. It seemed as if nobody had made him do it. The act was purely voluntary. We could not understand it. But there it was. Belle had a lovely new dress and she went to the dance. She blossomed. Something mysterious had simply happened to both of them, and they began to go everywhere together.

Belle began to talk and laugh and carry on like the rest of us. Chuck would wait for her in the corridor in time to walk home with her; that was a wonder in itself, besides all of the dates they had and the dances they went to. The rest of us were as pleased as if it had happened to one of us.

One day I saw the two of them going down the campus hill ahead of me. They were holding hands and swinging the hands between them in light-hearted camaraderie. But, when they came to the corner near Belle's house they stopped and stood still, looking into each other's eyes. He kissed her hastily and turned back, then Belle went on alone. Neither of them saw me and I went on my own way, but I thought to myself, "This is Mrs. Williams' doing."

Another day I saw Belle walking alone and I caught up with her. When I came near her I was sorry that I had, for I could see that she had been crying. It was too late to draw back now, so I said, "Belle, what's the matter?"

"Oh," she said, "I'm really miserable. Walk a little way and I'll tell you. I haven't told anyone, but maybe it'll help if I do. Mama won't let Chuck come to the house anymore. If anyone tells her that we've been seen together, she raises this awful row."

"But why?" I said. "Chuck is so nice. What's wrong with him?"

"She says he isn't good enough for me. Oh, that's a laugh! Not good enough for me. As if I were worth anything without him."

"What about your father?" I asked. "Isn't he on your side?"

"Oh, yes, I think he is. But he won't say anything to her. He knows how she'll explode. He can't bear stirring up trouble. I have to do it myself if anything is done."

"Oh, Belle," I said, "it's your life, not hers. Don't let her ruin everything for you—if you really love him."

"I do," she said. "I really love him, but I don't know if he loves me enough to go against her. If I lose him now, I'll die." She began to cry again.

We walked a long way together and I did not have much comfort or encouragement to offer. Only I was beginning to be a rebel myself and I kept telling her that she must live her own life.

"I know I must," she said. "But Mama has told me what I should do ever since I was born. I'm really frightened now."

I had no chance to talk with Belle alone again, but I saw with approval that during the last week of school she suddenly moved into the sorority house. She came with only the clothes on her back, and she had to go out to buy a toothbrush and other small necessities. She did not have much money either, and girls at the chapter house lent her dresses. We were all proud that she had asserted her independence. She held her small head high on the long, curved neck. She was friendly to everyone, but she did not explain herself. It was rumored, however, that her mother was furious with her and would not even accept the kindly intervention of her father.

It was an old sorority custom that on the last Saturday night before commencement the engaged girls announced the fact by running around the table between the main course and dessert. Their young men usually sent flowers or a large box of candy. We all waited in suspenseful excitement for the moment when the romantic secrets would be revealed.

On this particular occasion we knew who most of the runners would be: Connie and Pete had gone together since they were freshmen, Libby and Tom were a foregone conclusion, Susan and Bill had quarreled and made up so many times that we were not sure of them until Susan ran. Then there was a pause. We could see Belle stirring in her seat. Then suddenly, in a borrowed dress, she pushed back her chair and ran. She passed a big box of chocolates that Chuck had provided. We all screamed with delight.

"Oh, Belle, how soon?" we cried.

"As soon as possible," she said. "Tomorrow maybe."

"Not a formal wedding?"

"Oh, no, the very simplest."

"Will we be invited?"

Belle shook her head regretfully. "I'm sorry," she said. "If we make it to a justice of the peace, we'll be lucky."

Belle made one almost fatal mistake. She went home to get her clothes. Perhaps it was not entirely for her clothes. Belle was a gentle, loving girl. Perhaps with an act so nearly accomplished she hoped that her mother would relent and give her consent. Chuck went with her to carry her bags and hopefully to receive the parental blessing.

Mrs. Williams met them at the door and began to scream at them. The neighbors all up and down the street could hear her. She would not let Chuck into the house, but Belle persuaded her to allow her to come in alone to pack her things. Didn't she know her mother better than that? But Belle was a trusting soul.

She hastily packed a few essential garments into a bag and took off the borrowed dress. All vulnerable in a plain white slip, she went into the bathroom before she put on her own suit. Things seemed to be going reasonably well. Her mother had let her pack her bag and lay out the clothes she would wear to go away on the train.

She was running the water in the basin to wash her face when Belle heard the click of the lock on the bathroom door. All wet and worried, she rushed to try the knob. The door was locked.

"Mother!" Belle called. "Mother! Let me out."

Mrs. Williams only laughed. "Not until you change your mind," she said. So they had come to a complete impasse. Through the bathroom door they screamed at each other. Neither would give an inch. The door was locked and the one window in the bathroom was high and small. Belle was dressed only in a white slip. Mrs. Williams was superbly triumphant. She had brought it off. She was still the mistress in her own house and Belle was still her property.

But Belle was gradually developing some of her mother's spunk. She pushed the laundry hamper under the high window and climbed up so that she could look out. There was Chuck waiting apprehensively on the corner. He looked at his watch and then at the house. He had not expected that the packing would take so long. Then he heard Belle rapping on the window, and saw her looking out and beckoning.

"Oh, Chuck!" she said, "you've got to help me out of here." One of her long legs was already over the window sill. All she needed was a couple strong, upreaching arms.

It was all over town the next day: how Belle Williams had squirmed through a tiny bathroom window and run away to get married, without any of her lovely clothes, in nothing but a white slip. Some people even felt sorry for Mrs. Williams because she had a thankless daughter. But we young ones felt only glee that Belle had made her escape.

And so Belle and Chuck were married and lived happily ever after—at least I think they did. I saw them briefly years later. They were still married, looking prosperous and happy.

I left my town soon after the elopement, and I never knew what happened to Mrs. Williams. Perhaps, when she no longer had Belle to feed upon, she withered up and blew away.

Carol Ryrie Brink in the popular middy outfit of the day.

This photo and all others in this photo section courtesy of the Latah County Historical Society, Moscow, Idaho.

Carol Ryrie Brink at about age 8.

Brink as a young woman.

Top left: The Watkins home in Moscow, Idaho, where Carol Brink lived with her grandmother and aunt after her mother's suicide in 1904.

Lower left: A publicity photo of Carol Brink taken by her publisher, the Macmillan Company, in about 1960.

Above: Carol Brink on the left with her pony and cart at the University of Idaho's annual May Day Fete. Her friend Lillian Carrithers is at the right.

Carol Ryrie Brink's father, Alexander Ryrie, was born in Thurso, Scotland, in 1865. He moved to Moscow, Idaho, in 1889 and served as mayor from 1897 to 1899.

Carol Brink's mother, Henrietta Watkins, was the eldest daughter of William and Caroline Watkins. She married Alexander Ryrie in 1893 and after his death married Nat Brown in 1902. She committed suicide in 1904.

Elsie Watkins Phiel was born in 1876, the second daughter of William and Caroline Watkins. Single most of her life, she helped raise Carol Ryrie Brink after the death of Carol's parents.

Carol Brink continued the family tradition of naming daughters Caroline. Clockwise from top, Caroline Elsie Watkins Phiel, Brink's aunt; Caroline Woodhouse Watkins, her grandmother; Nora Caroline Brink, her daughter; and Carol Ryrie Brink.

Raymond "Blinky" Brink taught mathematics at the University of Idaho in the early 1900s. After marrying Carol, he spent most of his teaching career at the University of Minnesota.

Carol Ryrie Brink with her uncle Donald Ryrie, who immigrated from Scotland with her father, Alexander.

Below: Isaac J. Cogswell, who taught Carol Brink music lessons in Moscow's McConnell Mansion, came to the University of Idaho in 1893 to establish a department of music, which he served as head.

Top right: William J. McConnell arrived in Moscow in 1878 at the age of 49. He became a United States Senator and served two terms as governor of the new state.

Lower right: The McConnell Mansion, now a museum, is pictured here with the orignial picket fence and front porch atrium.

Top left: Dr. Francis J. Ledbrooke came to Moscow after the 1901 murder of the town's other physician, Carol Brink's grandfather William Watkins. He rented Watkins's office and took over the Watkins practice until his own suicide in 1902. The Watkins murder and the Ledbrooke/Booth suicides are key elements in Brink's novel *Buffalo Coat*.

Lower left: Winnifred Booth, the daughter of Methodist minister Rev. G. M. Booth, was the model for the character Jennie Walden in *Buffalo Coat*. In 1902 she committed suicide with Dr. Ledbrooke.

Above: James A. MacLean became president of the University of Idaho in 1900 and served until 1913.

Moscow, Idaho, in the 1890s.

25

Edward VIII

IF I COULD CLAIM Edward VIII of England I would really have a name to drop. I fell in love with him when I was thirteen, but alas! he never knew. In 1908 my grandfather in Scotland sent me a large, white-covered book called *Queen Alexandra's Christmas Gift Book, Photographs from My Camera*. It was a book with great snob appeal, sold for charity, to the masses of the British public, who, in those days, seemed happiest when they were living vicariously the glamorous lives of their nobility.

The book is made up of photographs, very simply captioned, "My Father and My Brother, Bernsdorff 1904," "Wilton Tea-party: Lord and Lady Lansdown, Lady de Grey, and Lord Pembroke," "The Lords of the Admiralty, Naval Review, 1907." About half the pictures are printed on glossy white paper; the others are real photographs pasted on black paper as in a family album.

This book of snapshots by a queen had a tremendous fascination for me. I pored over it by the hour, getting to know in a familiar way the little princes and princesses whose destinies seemed immutable, whose fates seemed to lie in the most pleasant of places. I turn the pages of this book today with a different sort of fascination. The safe and tidy world of 1908 has vanished from the earth.

The first picture in the book is a memorable one: "The King, George and His Two Sons." A portly Edward VII in admiral's hat stands looking to sea on the royal yacht while beside him a bearded man gazes with fatherly concern at two bright-eyed little boys in sailor suits and caps—four kings, as it turned out, although no one could have foretold that the youngest boy would be king also, and perhaps the best of the four.

Then there is "Little Olav," toddling in a long white coat and round white hat tied with ribbons under his chin, taken in 1905, and later in sweater and large straw hat, taken with his father, Haakon of Norway. His life has followed the expected pattern more nearly than any of the others.

Among the pictures that I loved best were those of the young grand duchesses of Russia. The eldest must have been about my age, and I had a ruffled white dress and a big white hat made of lace and chiffon something like theirs — only theirs were much more elegant than mine. The honest Slavic faces, just short of being beautiful, look out hopefully beneath the monstrous hats, and all the world of wealth, privilege, and honor seems to spread ahead of them. The little Czarevitch in sailor costume, heir to the throne of all the Russias, stands erect and resolute beside his "sailor friend." In Idaho we were as certain as they must have been that life would follow its accustomed course. How could we guess what tempest clouds were gathering?

And "Little David," Prince of Wales, was the best of all! Born a year before I was, I gazed with romantic eyes at the handsome, schoolboy face under the naval officer's cap. In one picture he looked out at me as if he were expecting me. In another, with medals on his short jacket, he is pulling on the hawser of the royal yacht while an officer in gold epaulettes and braid with white gloves and a sword stands at respectful attention.

It was then that I fell in love with "Little David." All things seemed possible to me, and, while I rode my pony over the Idaho hills, I built a wonderful romance for little David and myself. I would be a beautiful young lady, going to visit my grandfather in Scotland. The Prince of Wales would be staying at Balmoral — yes, there were many pictures in Queen Alexandra's gift book of Balmoral castle, and nobody told me that, although it was in Scotland, it was many miles from the humble croft where my grandfather raised oats and turnips and burned the peat he cut from his own land in the cold wind from the North Sea. I would be riding out on a spirited horse (there were always spirited horses in my dreams), then the Prince would see me, and — well, I had been nourished on fairy stories, so the rest was simply routine. The Prince and Princess would ride away into the sunset to live happily ever after. I never dreamed that he might abdicate for me. I wouldn't have asked it of him. I would have been content to retire to a nunnery with the serene conviction that I had aroused his deathless devotion.

I soon outgrew my dreams, seeing, reluctantly, the unsuitability of my humble self as Queen of England. I wouldn't have understood the protocol; I'm sure I wouldn't have liked cutting ribbons and dedicating hospitals. Yet I was always a little jealous of Wally Simpson. She was unsuitable, too, and she let him abdicate. The only time I ever heard his voice was as it came resolutely over the wireless: "For the woman I love." So he wasn't just a picture in an old album. He was a man, and his love led him to extravagant decisions. Later I saw his deeply lined face and vacant eyes in jet-set news releases, and I was sorry for him.

It is, after all, better to be unimportant in this world. I have survived where all those beautiful, noble people have met violence and disillusion and annihilation.

Yet I am sure that I loved Edward VIII before Wally did. The difference between us was that she did something about it and I didn't.

26

McKinley Helm

IF YOU LOOK UP the State of Idaho in the yearly Almanac you will find a tabulation of information: capital: Boise; governor: (current); state flower: syringa; state tree: white pine; state song: "Here We Have Idaho."

The state song is also the official song of the University of Idaho. When I stand to sing this song my mind goes back a long way, beyond the memories of the people who stand around me and sing more lustily than I as I rarely raise my voice in lusty song because I am sure to be off key. But with this song there are other considerations that keep me silent. I am filled with surprise that people still sing it, as my nostalgic emotions are stirred because I was present at the first public singing and I knew the author.

When I was a sophomore in college I had been placed on the song committee for the annual competition of class skits and songs. I was angry because in my freshman year two friends and I had written and produced the prize-winning skit or "stunt" as we used to call it. This year my two friends were put on the stunt committee and I was put on the song committee. I don't remember who was responsible for assigning our positions, but, in retrospect, there seems to have been no recourse. I hated music and I adored humor. The stunts were full of humor; the songs were deadly serious, filled with "loving alma maters" and noble yearnings. The result was that I withdrew in haughty disdain to let the other members of the sophomore committee write the song. I can't remember a thing about our song except that it did not win.

That year a rather strange young man had entered the university as a junior English major, a transfer from some other college. He belonged to one of the fraternities, but otherwise he seemed to be a deviation from the norm, the unforgivable creative in any youthful society: the non-conformist. He was small and rather gaudily dressed. He was a wonderful dancer, although he had a mincing walk. It was said that he wrote poetry, and such a rumor immediately set him beyond the pale. It was even reported that he had written a poem about me. It seems that someone passing him in the hall had heard him declaiming: "Carol, every violet has / Heaven for a looking glass!" This caused great mirth. I was not perturbed. I knew that the lines were part of the epilogue to *The Flower of Old Japan* by Alfred Noyes, a poem now long forgotten but then a favorite in English departments.

The Flower of Old Japan had been given to me by a friend with whom I was deeply involved but who was far away. Blinky was neither poet nor English department hound, but the name had caught his fancy, and on the page which Noyes dedicates "To Carol, a Little Maiden of Miyako," Blinky had put a card which said, "To Carol, a Little Maiden of the West."

But Blinky was at Harvard and I was very much alive in Idaho, a long way away.

The name of the new young man in the junior class was McKinley Helm. He was clever and smart and had sufficient vitality to be himself, in spite of the fact that he did not conform to any of the patterns. The football players, who were all brawn and little brain, jeered at him; the professors approved of him because he was brilliant, witty, and well-prepared in class; the girls loved dancing with him, but, because the football heroes jeered, they felt compelled to titter at him afterwards.

I had danced with him once or twice in those marvelous old-fashioned parties when everybody danced with everybody else and "going steady" was unheard of, unless you happened to be engaged to be married. It was a time of fun and gaiety and utter lightheartedness, before the long shadow of the First World War cast its gloom over a hither-to innocent generation. Pansies were still pansies to us and fairies were fairies. I don't think that McKinley was "queer" in the way that, today, we imagine every non-conformist who dances and writes poetry to be. I got to know him very well and to be fond of him.

But that first year he was the popular freak of the campus. He was asked to write the junior class song.

The evening of the interclass competition arrived. I watched with envy the stunt preparations of my sophomore friends and with scorn the feeble attempts of the sophomore song writers. I wanted the sophomore stunt to win, even if I wasn't in it, because we had set the pattern last year and my two best girl friends were involved again this year.

The night of the contest the auditorium was crowded and scintillating with partisan spirit. A competitive stunt was followed by a competitive song. There were faculty judges and wildly applauding backers of each class effort. The sophomores won nothing. This year the juniors swept the field.

The junior stunt was something about a harem, and they had inveigled McKinley Helm into dressing as Scheherazade in harem pantaloons with bare midriff, many strings of pearls, a wig and a veil over nose and chin. He was good-humored and he loved a gag, but the skit was cruel to him; in fact, every one of the four stunts lampooned him savagely.

There is no place for bitterness and cruelty in humor. Satire may be cruel and biting in its way, but the sting should be softened by intelligence and a handsome style. Humor should above all things be good-natured. That year the humor of the stunts was uniformly crude and malicious: a mincing parody of McKinley Helm paraded through each one of them. But his song, "Here We Have Idaho," won the song prize for the juniors. I don't think that he had written the music, and the words were not particularly distinguished, but somehow the combination was appealing.

After the performances I stopped to talk to friends and much of the crowd had left the auditorium before I did. So I was there when McKinley came down the side steps from the stage. He was all alone. He had changed from the harem bloomers and pearls into a dress suit. (Yes, they wore them in college in those days.) And he was all alone. No one in his stunt accompanied him. The audience in going out had turned its back on him. No one came forward to congratulate him. If he had been an oddball before, this horrible performance had permanently labeled him the college oddity. I had been lonely myself and had felt myself the odd one in the laughing horde. I was usually shy about making advances, but now I hurried among the empty seats to intercept him. I ran and put myself in front of him.

"It was wonderful!" I said. "The song was wonderful. Congratulations! It deserved to win."

The blank look of desperation faded from his eyes and gradually the lighthearted twinkle began to return.

"You mean it?" he said.

"Yes, I do. You ought to be very proud."

We stood looking at each other awkwardly, but with growing understanding.

"Would you –" he said. "I mean, I wonder, would you – maybe – *could you* – go to the movies with me on Friday night?"

"Friday night?" I said vaguely, my mind not really clicking as to whether I had a previous date or not. I knew I would go. "Yes, I think I could. You know where I live?"

"Yes, I know," he said. "You're the girl who has the pony cart."

I suppose I was a laughingstock myself, because I was nearly twenty still driving a fat Iceland pony to a two-wheeled cart. Some of my boyfriends wouldn't have been caught dead in the pony cart, but others rather relished the distinction and amusement of riding around in it.

McKinley became one of the chief riders. I hope I did something to restore him to the status of a normal human being. I don't think that he was ever bitterly lampooned again while he was in college. They had done their worst to him on that dreadful evening and perhaps the crudeness of the humor had even turned the stomachs of the brawny, brainless ones.

But whatever good I may have done to him, he did infinitely more for me in the way of novelty and entertainment. He had a compassionate sense of humor and an infinite variety of zany ideas that fitted my own. We couldn't see my grandmother's old garden hat and work apron hanging up in the kitchen without suddenly becoming hillbilly farmers and going to call on all of our friends in character. We stole overripe ears of field corn from a country field and roasted them over a small bonfire while the moon rose over the hill. We labored over poetry for the Sans Souci Club. We walked the railroad tracks in spring for pussy willows and sat on the gravestones in the cemetery while we talked philosophy. And we danced and danced. When we went on double dates with more amorous and less adventurous couples who were content to roll into a blanket and lie inert, we composed limericks or invented a new language, or tried out the swings in some country schoolyard. It was the best kind of fun.

When he left for the summer he paid me a dollar for a subscription to a correspondence service and I wrote him a weekly letter in any character that came into my head: Theda Barracuda, the movie star; Tutti-Fruiti, the Japanese girl; or little Mabel, the child prodigy. He wrote back long, lonesome letters from the cemetery where he had got a job as maintenance man, a cemetery without the consolation of philosophical discourse. His father had a small variety store in a neighboring town. I think that McKinley must have been an intellectual freak in his own family, for I'm sure that they were all resolutely, solidly respectable middle-class. The only member of his family that I ever met was a much older sister who was sent up to inspect me because the family were fearful that he might conceivably be falling in love, and how in the world was he going to support a wife?

He was very worried and apologetic about the sister's coming. Her ostensible reason for coming was to hear a missionary who was to speak to the college YWCA. I was snobbishly scornful of the drab girls who belonged to the college YWCA, and they were not McKinley's "cup of tea" either. But his sister was determined to the extent of bringing her little boy with her.

It would have been nice for me to have invited her and her little boy for Sunday dinner at Gram's, but Aunt would have none of it. Aunt, on her side, was worried that I might be falling in love with McKinley. It was quite ridiculous, because the two of us were simply having a marvelous time together without a serious intention in our heads.

The lady came, a humorless little woman with thick-lensed glasses and a long Polish name that I never entirely mastered. Her little boy was about three, very pale and spiritless. McKinley took us to dinner at a cafe, a thing almost unheard of in our town on a

Sunday when everybody should be eating at home. Mrs. Long-Polish-Name asked me all sorts of leading questions while McKinley sat in agonized silence on the other side of the table. The little boy wanted more mashed potatoes, and, as I didn't care for mine, he sat on my lap and ate mine out of my dish. Later on the mashed potatoes all came up and were dealt with by our combined napkins.

I had not seen a more stricken look on McKinley's face since the night of the song and stunt competition. I went with his sister to the YWCA meeting while McKinley paced the pavement outside. She gave me the baby to hold while she went up to talk to the missionary, and the baby fell asleep in my arms. I wouldn't have minded except that some of the drab YWCA girls insisted in giggling.

After the minister went home, we resumed our thoughtless gaiety. But some of the spontaneity had gone out of it. There was a real world somewhere beyond the make-believe one. Sensible people were worried about us.

He graduated and got a job as a cub reporter for a Spokane newspaper. We saw each other irregularly, meeting at the houses of friends, exchanging kisses, wondering if anything could be worked out on a permanent basis. But most of the magic had gone, and always, always at the back of my mind there was Blinky: tall, dark, devoted, with all the things that McKinley was not and never, never would be.

During the war McKinley went overseas as an ambulance driver, and I am afraid I was guilty of writing him a "Dear John" letter when Blinky came out to see me.

After the war he had a scholarship at Oxford or Cambridge, I don't remember which. For a time he was an Anglican priest. Then I heard that he had met an heiress on a train. They were married, and it was reported to me by college friends who visited them in Boston that they dined in state every evening in formal evening attire sitting at opposite ends of a long table and waited upon by well-trained servants.

McKinley became an authority on Mexican and other modern art. He wrote books about Mexican art and a monograph on John Marin. He was a pioneer in appreciation of the contribution of the Negro and published a book on Roland Hayes who was his friend.

He also wrote a book about Father Junipero Serra, and a delightful travel book, called *Spring in Spain,* which detailed his travels with his wife and two Pekinese dogs and a large box of books.

Some years later my husband and I occupied the same room which McKinley had occupied and described in the *Parador del Condestable Davalos* in Ubeda.

I never saw or corresponded with him again, but I heard of him through friends. He died comparatively young of a heart attack.

I suppose that for the most part his books have now been lost in the competitive shuffle of changing times and are rarely read. But the song, the one surviving song of all those written during the years of song competitions, "Here We Have Idaho," still goes on and probably will for generations. Things work out oddly sometimes. But, whenever I hear people sing it, I am filled with nostalgic memories.

27

Katherine Lowry and the Indians

WHEN KATHERINE LOWRY stayed with us the young Indian seminary students from Lapwai used to come to call on her. They came early and they sat late; they spoke not at all. They were solid, good-looking young men with coal-black hair, smooth bronze skins, high cheek bones, and prominent noses. They wore decent black business suits. The Nez Perces are handsome people of an unsurpassed dignity and calm.

Katherine's aunts and great aunts, as missionaries to the Indians on the Lapwai reservation, had for more than a generation been turning the fine, upstanding young men into Presbyterian ministers, elders, and deacons. Whenever one of these young men had business in our town, Aunt Mazie Crawford would say, "Be sure to look up my niece Katherine while you are there."

Sometimes we fed the men dinner, but often they came after dinner and sat, silent rocks of decorum, answering "yes" and "no" to our questions, utterly without self-conscious embarrassment over the long conversational lapses. Grandma smiled and retired early. She had known Indians in her youth; she respected them and never pushed them. I was quiet myself. I took my school books to the dining-room table to do my homework. But Katherine and Aunt stayed valiantly on in the parlor, prodding their brains for suitable questions.

"Is Aunt Mazie well?"

"Yes."

"Is the weather good?"

"No."

"Do you like pumpkin pie?"

Grunt.

The Indians smiled. They were sociably inclined, but they saw no need for words. Katherine was nearly as nervous a conversationalist as my aunt, but gradually her inventiveness lagged. Only my aunt went on and on.

"Was your father a great chief?"

"No."

"Do you remember Chief Joseph?"

"No."

"Do you still eat camas roots?"

"No."

"Do you have many dogs?"

"Yes."

"Ponies?"

"No."

Sometimes she tried to trick them by asking questions that could not be answered by yes or no.

"What will you do when you are ordained a Presbyterian minister?"

Grunt.

It was no use.

Usually about midnight the silent guests arose, shook hands ceremoniously, and departed as silently as they had come. Then, clutching each other in mock despair, Aunt and Katherine would stagger into the dining room where I was still at my books.

"Oh, my patience!" Katherine would cry. "They're very nice, but why does Aunt Mazie send them?"

"She wants them to learn the social graces no doubt," said Aunt.

"But how will they ever preach a sermon? Can you imagine?"

"Maybe they are more fluent in Nez Perce," I suggested.

"Oh, my patience! Oh, my patience!" It was one of Katherine's favorite expressions, as it contained all her wonder and amusement at an incomprehensible world.

She was a very thin, bright, tense young woman, full of amiability and ready laughter. Some nice young man should have looked at her seriously a long time ago. She was worth looking at. She had curly dark hair with only a thread or two here and there of premature gray; her dark eyes were unnaturally bright and sparkling. She was warm and loving. How nice she would have been with children! But she came of a line of Spartan spinsters, valiant ladies full of sturdy courage and spirit. Although some of the valiant spirit was still there, the sturdiness had grown thin in Katherine. Her mother had made the mistake of being married and dying young. The Valkyrie strain was running out.

The Lapwai Indian reservation is, or perhaps I should say was, a very interesting place. When I saw it after the deaths of the Crawford sisters it was run down and seedy. There was a small dark museum, and school buildings little used and falling into disrepair. Where were the Indians? No one told me what had become of them.

The history of the Lapwai Indian mission goes back to 1837 when the Whitmans and the Spaldings traveled across the continent to bring the Word of God to the Indians. It really goes back farther than that to the time in 1831 when four natives of the Nez Perce tribe arrived in St. Louis to ask the white men to send them teachers to tell them about the white man's God, who, they had heard, was more powerful than any of their own gods.

The Whitmans and the Spaldings were the answer to this plea. Both men were married and they took their wives with them. Narcissa Whitman and Eliza Spalding were the first white women ever to cross the prairies and wilderness to reach the Oregon Territory. Narcissa was a vigorous, healthy, and beautiful woman; her husband, Marcus, was a strong man, a doctor as well as a preacher, and already experienced in pioneering. Henry Spalding was a less impressive man who had proposed to Narcissa and been rejected; his wife, Eliza, was so very ill on the six-month journey westward that at one time she begged them to go on and leave her to die along on the prairie. Yet the Spaldings had some kind of stamina and good sense that was enduring, and they chose to go with the Nez Perce to form the mission at Lapwai.

The Whitmans chose the Cayuse Indians and established their mission at Waiilatpu, near the present town of Walla Walla, Washington. Whitman made the mistake of expecting too much of them. He believed that he could not accept them as Christians until they understood the doctrines of the church as fully as the civilized white Christians did. The Cayuse were proud, and they felt that he was withholding something from them and making the way of Christianity too hard. As other white settlers arrived they brought diseases with them to which the Indians had no immunity. When the white people recovered from an epidemic of measles and many of the Indians died, the Cayuse blamed Whitman's "medicine" and felt that he had poisoned them. This led in 1847 to the massacre in which both Marcus and Narcissa were killed along with fourteen other white people.

The Spaldings' little daughter, Eliza, one of the first white children born west of the Rockies, was staying at the Whitman mission at the time of the massacre, but she was one of those who lived to recount the horrors of a bloody day.

At Lapwai the Spaldings were easy with the Indians, and the Nez Perce were helpful and friendly. They said of Mrs. Spalding that she had a "quiet heart." Some of the Indians accepted Christianity and began to settle into the pattern of living that the missionaries offered them. If the white man had dealt fairly with them they would have made good citizens. But it was beyond the power of the missionaries to regulate the greed of other white men. Treaties were made and broken, gold was discovered in nearby Orofino, and many of the Indians were driven off their home lands.

The lady of the quiet heart died, and Henry Spalding left the region for twenty-four years. When he returned in 1871 he had only three years to live. But the missionary board sent him a helper in the person of Miss Sue McBeth who came as a teacher in the government school in 1873. She was Katherine Lowry's great aunt. Physically she was as frail and sickly as Eliza Spalding had been, but she had a soul and will of granite.

It is interesting that the history of the relationship of the Nez Perce people to whites, one of the least ignoble chapters in our dealings with the Indians, was dominated by a series of fragile but determined white women: Eliza Spalding, Sue and her sister Kate McBeth, a Miss Alice C. Fletcher who was sent by the government to supervise the allotting of land to the individual Indians in 1895 and who was noted for her clemency and good judgment, and finally the Crawford sisters, who were nieces of the McBeths. These women wielded a tremendous influence over the Indians and were revered as teachers and tribal mothers. I think that no man could have managed so well.

Great conversions were made. The Christian Indians gave up the feathers and animal tails which symbolized their attending spirits or *Wy-ya-kin,* and put on the white man's clothing. Those who remained wild were called blanket Indians because they still wore the blankets and war paint and still indulged in gambling, racing, drinking, and wife swapping. There were great Fourth of July celebrations at which the blanket Indians whooped it up, while the Christian Indians encamped in the church yard next door to sing psalms and pray. Somehow the small white mothers made hymn singing and praying exciting enough to draw more and more of the Indians to their side of the fence.

But men far away in Washington made the ultimate decisions, and the famous war of Chief Joseph grew out of the breaking of an 1855 treaty which had given the Nez Perces land "where they would never again be disturbed while the sun shone or the water ran." The new treaty, only twelve years later, was destined to deprive them of much of this same land. It took away that part of the reserve lying north of the Snake and Clearwater Rivers, and the beautiful Wallowa Valley which Chief Joseph considered his own. He cherished the broad valley where the kous and camas roots, that formed so much of the Nez Perce food supply, grew. When the camas blossomed, it was blue as flax and spread across the valley floor like a gently waving inland sea. Around it rose low mountains, one beyond another, clothed in pines that were a darker shade of blue as they receded into the distance. There the game was to be found, and in the river there were fish. It was a good land and it had been promised to them while the sun shone and the water ran.

About fifty of the Christian and some of the wiser Nez Perces signed the new treaty, realizing that rebellion was useless. Chiefs Joseph, White Bird, and Looking Glass refused to give up their lands, so the tribe was split in two. It is not necessary to go into the familiar epic of Chief Joseph's brave stand, his defeat, and the long and tragic attempt to lead his people to Canada. He was perhaps the greatest of all Indian leaders, and the story of his defeat is a heartbreaking one.

But the Christian missions at Lapwai and Kamiah continued to flourish. The McBeth sisters were wise enough to train up the Indian men to be ministers and elders in their own churches, so that, even in a new religion, they remained the leaders of their people. The two good women taught sewing and cooking and household skills to the women, as well as Christian doctrine to the men. Their little houses were centers of service and activity, practical as well as spiritual. The hardships were great and sometimes their lives were threatened by the unconverted Indians, but they went on serenely in the certainty that the Lord would provide and protect. They continued the work, begun by the Spaldings, of translating the Bible and familiar hymns into the Nez Perce language. The Indians loved to sing. It was one of the greatest attractions of their new-found faith.

When Sue McBeth, who had been born on the banks of the Doon in Scotland, died on the banks of the Clearwater in Idaho, she was sixty years of age. Her death occurred on a Saturday in May of 1893, and, since they had been taught not to bury on the Sabbath day, the Indians placed her body on the platform of the pulpit where it remained throughout the regular services of the day. The people crowded the church weeping and saying, "The mother has gone. We are orphans now." She was buried beside the little church in Kamiah that she had organized.

During the years in Kamiah and Lapwai, Miss Sue McBeth had compiled a dictionary of 15,000 Nez Perce words, together with grammar, and had translated most of the Bible and many hymns into the native tongue. After her death her manuscripts were put into a box to be sent to the Smithsonian Institution in Washington. The first part of the journey was in a steamboat on the Snake River. The steamboat, the *Annie Faxon,* blew up fifty miles below Lewiston, killing everyone on board. It was thought that everything was lost. A former Lapwai man, who lived on a farm some miles below the scene of the accident, happened to be riding near the river and noticed debris from the wrecked boat floating on the water. A red box caught his eye. He waded his horse as far out in the river as he could, threw his lasso and caught the box just as it was going over some rapids. Inside was Miss McBeth's bulky manuscript, damp but still decipherable. On hearing of this, one of her elders said, "It seems as if that box was a living thing, and that the Lord was caring for it."

Katherine used to tell us about the wonderful summer camp meetings that she sometimes attended, where Nez Perces gathered from many miles around to pitch their teepees and tether their ponies and sing hymns and pray. The little woman from Scotland had managed to make Christianity a gay and happy thing.

When I was a child I used to see Miss Kate McBeth. She would come down to Presbytery accompanied by her grave and dignified ministers and elders. She often stayed with us because we were just across the street from the Presbyterian church, and my grandmother had a great respect for her. She was a small, dumpy woman in old-fashioned dark clothing, probably culled from a missionary barrel. It was the missionary barrels that furnished most of the jackets and trousers that had supplanted the blankets for the Christian Indians. Kate McBeth was an unimpressive figure; nevertheless, she had an aura of authority and well-organized power. I felt the electric magnetism radiating around her. She had never asked unreasonable things of her Nez Perces—only that they should go out and minister to their own people in a reverent and appropriate way.

When Kate began to feel her powers failing she sent for her niece, Mazie Crawford, another spinster with the McBeth touch and resolution. There was a second Crawford sister, too, named Elizabeth. The thick red blood of the McBeth sisters had been considerably thinned in their nieces. Still these were valiant, capable women; the kind, understanding work of the mission churches went on. The Crawfords also used to visit us and they were gracious, upright women, less Spartan perhaps, but still a mighty power. One could think of them as Presbyterian nuns, dedicated to religious service.

When they brought Katherine west from Ohio they must have hoped and prayed that possibly, by some divine miracle, she would carry on the work when the Lord called them to lay it down.

"Oh, my patience!" cried Katherine. "I haven't any of the proper qualities. I couldn't—oh, I couldn't!"

She had a job as a secretary in our town, and she laughed and ran up and down the hills and was delighted by all the wonders of the world. We loved her and cherished her, but a Spartan leader she was not. I possess a copy of Kate McBeth's book, *The Nez Perces Since Lewis and Clark,* and I prize it because it is inscribed in a tremulous, old-woman's hand to my grandmother from "K. C. McBeth" on "Oct. 12th 1914." I read in it courage, resolution, love, practical Christianity, and good sense. The book was copyrighted in 1908 and I have no later record to bring me up to date on the Nez Perces.

But still I hear the seemingly interminable monologues in the parlor and see the amiable young Indians sitting straight up in their chairs and smiling. If we had only asked them to sing!

"Were the crops good this year?"

"Yes."

"How many bushels to the acre?"

Grunt.

"Do you have any brothers and sisters?"

"Yes."

"How many?"

Grunt.

And then the ceremonious shaking of hands, the closing of the front door, and Katherine and my aunt collapsing on the dining room couch.

"Oh, my patience!"

28

Nora

NORA HAD WEAK ankles and she was slightly overweight. If we went to a meeting of the Ladies' Uplift Society for Fallen Women, she was likely to turn an ankle and fall all the way down the aisle in the midst of shocked onlookers. I learned to take her arm and keep a steady hand on her elbow. We went to everything that amused us whether it uplifted or knocked down. Our curiosity about the marvelous world was insatiable. We wanted to see and do everything, a large ambition for human beings bound by a normal lifespan. That her life was to be briefer than most we fortunately did not know.

We saw each other first at a crowded sorority rush party, and some gleam of the eye or quirk of the lip united us in a common bond of detached amusement. We both came from quiet, introspective households; all this noise of social busy-ness confused and amazed us. But it did not flabbergast us. We still had a sense of the ludicrous and we could laugh. How we laughed over the years we knew each other! I have never laughed so exquisitely and well with anyone since – or before. We loved each other because we could laugh so well together. I still believe that women can love women and men, men, without the sticky implications of perversity. We loved each other dearly and we could talk about any subject in the world without constraint or hindrance. Perfect ease and understanding: isn't that, after all, what friendship is?

Nora Ashton was a very blond, small English girl who had come to America with her father, mother, sister, and brother when she was twelve years old. She still had a delicate hint of English purity in her precise enunciation and pleasant diction. Her father was a bookkeeper in Nampa, Idaho, and a lay minister in the Episcopal

Church. He was grave and serious, and reminded me of my own father with his sandy moustache, gentle blue eyes, and dedication to religion and the hope of a better world. I think the gleam of mischief and wonder in Nora's eyes came from her mother, a tall, dark woman who loved books, was vague and incompetent as a housekeeper, but always ready to laugh with a couple of laughing girls. There was something monstrously wrong with the family health. Mrs. Ashton suffered from a debilitating form of heart disease, and the other daughter became a wheelchair invalid for most of her life. As to Nora—but that was a long way ahead of us. When we first met she seemed as sturdy as anyone, except for the treacherous ankles.

The Ashtons had a very limited income and Nora, when she came to college, brought a trunk almost empty of possessions, but a head well stocked with English literature both classical and modern together with an enthusiasm for Latin. The love of Latin amazed us all. I had "ponied" my way through what Latin was then required in high school for entrance into an accredited college, and I detested it. "A dead language!" I said scornfully. She opened her blue eyes wide. "But, Caroline Sybil," she said, making gentle fun of my full name, "Latin is the basis of so much of our everyday language. That makes it interesting, don't you see?" At her suggestion I later went with her to a course on appreciation of Greek and Roman civilizations and found that the little "dry as dust" professor could open a wonderful door to an unknown world of riches.

But to return to her trunk—Nora had a simple basic wardrobe that she had been able to assemble with thrift and foresight. She wore a peculiar, greenish-striped wool coat with a cape, like an old English coaching coat; she had a black evening dress. In my era of college no girl ever wore a *black* evening dress—pale green, pale blue, pale pink, even yellow, but never, never black. What freak of economy had given Nora a black evening dress, I don't know, but her extreme blondness was suited to it. She looked very well.

She came up to college with a "boyfriend" of high school days who had played Shawn to her Marie in a high school production of *The Land of Heart's Desire*. He was moody, arty, and talented. They were one of the couples in the Sans Souci Club and everyone assumed that they were destined for each other, but somewhere along the way they became unstuck. The man she finally married was of quite a different stamp.

During our first year of college we had a hand in most of the sorority and college stunts and playlets. The sorority house was then an incredible old building, yet it still housed students when I visited my town fifty years later. It seemed to be a derelict when we occupied it, and the sisterhood has built and lived in two new houses since the days when we were young. What miracle of paint and plaster and glue has kept the old house going is a mystery to me.

I lived across town and only crowded into the sorority house during initiation week or on special occasions, but I became familiar with the tiny rooms into which two or three girls were crowded. In winter the rooms were heated by small metal stoves. There was a large, outdoor sleeping porch where narrow beds were lined up in rows as in a hospital or an orphanage, and sometimes in winter the occupants of the beds awoke to find snow on their pillows.

Nora shared a room with a delightfully puckish girl named Verna, and the three of us used to sit around the stove exchanging wisecracks and laughing enormously. Our playlet won first place for the freshman class in the annual competition, and we were usually responsible for the sorority skits and entertainments. During initiation week we suffered together. According to sorority decree we had to make the paddles which would be used on us during our ordeal, so we not only made the paddles but burned what we considered smart remarks into them with a hot poker: *"If seniors come, can blows be far behind?" "Spare the rod, the child is already spoiled." "Forward into battle." "Help!"*

We had much to laugh about. All of us girls wore one or two ample petticoats under our dresses. At the annual May Day festival when the various gym classes danced in costume on the greensward and the freshmen girls wound a Maypole, Nora lost her petticoat during the winding of the Maypole. The petticoat was rather casually gathered around her waist with a draw string. During the dancing, with a crowd of college and townspeople looking on, Nora heard an ominous snap and felt the petticoat coming down. Some of us with alarm saw it emerging beneath the green cambric costume of

the Maypole dancer. There was nothing we could do. With a pause
in the dance the Maypole ribbons would have been inextricably tan-
gled. I thought of Nora's weak ankles and the ever-increasing ex-
panse of white petticoat. But Nora met the situation superbly. When
the petticoat reached her ankles, she caught it up, draped it over
her arm, and never missed a step in the dance.

Then there was the time during a vacation period when one
of the sorority seniors asked Nora to prepare link sausages for lunch.
"But how do you link sausages?" Nora asked innocently.

It is a pleasure to remember a time when everything was so
funny, and every door was open. The doors close one by one. I wish
every young person such a season of unreasoning lightheartedness,
and a friend to share it.

One time when most of our friends had dates for a college dance
and Nora and I did not, we formed what we called the Broken Heart
or BH Society. It was dedicated to the proposition that we should
not sit around and feel sorry for ourselves, but should go out and
find a more intriguing adventure than the one we were missing. I
can't remember what we did that first time. It all began so care-
lessly. But BH came to mean something very definite to us, so much
so that I still get a life of heart when I see the two initials in some
other context. It meant to us looking around at the wonderful world
and drinking it in like wine; it meant going out of our way to meet
adventure no matter how inconspicuous it might seem; it meant conscious participation in life.

We only admitted one other member into our BH Society. That
was Blinky, who was to become my husband. Nora was generous
enough to agree that he was BH, and we made him an honorary
member. When she wrote to me later about her own impending marriage she told me how handsome, interesting, and good he was, but
then she said in a small aside, "But, Carol, he isn't BH." Perhaps
she hoped to train him.

Our BH adventures were really small ones, such as hitchhiking
our way from Nora's home in Nampa to Boise to visit friends. Hitchhiking was an almost unknown art in those days, and I remember
we made the trip in three stages by farm wagon, by delivery cart,
and by automobile. Another chance adventure found us in borrowed

clothes attending the queen of the county fair when she presented a collar of roses to the winner of the horse race. Everything we did had a BH flavor or intent, and everything reeked with laughter.

At the end of Nora's sophomore year her money gave out and she spent the next year teaching a one-room country school while I went on to finish my junior year. We exchanged endless letters full of lofty thoughts and down-to-earth daily adventures, hopes, and frustrations.

> Dear Sister BH:
> How do you cope with twenty restless kids of all ages and grades of intelligence? I'm not cut out to be a school marm really. "Heaven is high and Hell is deep and life is a worship of sorrows" — Sartor Resartus by Thomas Carlyle (Don't read it! It's not all that good.) Write me something exciting. I faint! I perish!
> N. A.

During that year we made a tremendous decision: the next year we would go to Berkeley to the University of California. It would not be much more expensive for Nora than going north to the University of Idaho, and she had carefully saved her money. We met in Portland, Oregon, and took one of the old coastal steamers to San Francisco. We were both seasick on the rough passage, but life was rosy again, the club was in session, and laughter was the order of the day.

The First World War had started, that jolly war to end all wars and make the world safe for democracy, and California was a truly BH place.

We were met in San Francisco by a Miss Unwin, a friend of Nora's family, a brisk lady who taught zoology at the university. She realized that she had two virtuous and unattended young girls on her hands, and she had secured a room for us with a Mrs. Lowden, and board across the street at St. Margaret's Hall. St. Margaret's Hall was a training school for Episcopalian girls run by deaconesses. I still remember how they looked: severe dark-haired ladies in glasses with neat blue uniforms and white caps. I didn't know whether we could stand this or not, but Miss Unwin was so kind that we hated to seem ungrateful. So we settled into a dark little room with a redeeming fireplace that was next to Mrs. Lowden's kitchen. We were not supposed to hang pictures on the walls but we did, and every day Mrs. Lowden came in while we were at school and took the pictures down, and every day when we returned from school we put them up again. Mrs. Lowden got her revenge by recounting, very loudly in the adjoining kitchen to her friend Miss Fricke, all of our shortcomings and scandalous behavior. We were not supposed to have a fire in the fireplace either, but, when we returned from a concert or entertainment in San Francisco or Berkeley, we took off our white gloves and foraged for scrap wood on vacant lots and had lovely fires in the fireplace.

We entertained Blinky here when he returned from France, and that scandalized Mrs. Lowden too, especially when we went with him for a weekend to Mt. Tamalpais and Muir Woods.

"They *may* be innocent," she said very loudly to Miss Fricke while we were in our beds in the next room, "but it's very, very compromising. They don't seem to care how things look to other people."

The food at St. Margaret's Hall was awful, and the girls were very dull. We investigated the possibilities of living at the sorority house, but at the first and only meeting we attended the girls were discussing how they would finance the new oriental rugs they were installing, and we beat a hasty retreat. This was not the sorority we knew with its snowy sleeping porch and small rooms with red hot pokes.

Our own finances were very shaky. When we returned home in June we were literally penniless. We had to fend off the services of the Pullman porter because we knew we couldn't tip him, and we went the last day without food. We savored this as something quite BH. Now we knew how the hungry lowest level of society felt. Or did we? We couldn't help anticipating that Aunt would have a good chicken dinner waiting for us when we arrived in Idaho, but we wrung as much profit as possible out of our poverty.

There was the time when we found, on a sidewalk in San Francisco, the bankbook of Miss Amelia L. Gates with a one-dollar bill folded into it. We thought that we could get more pleasure out of one dollar than Miss Amelia L. Gates could, so we decided to see how far we could make it go. Our idea was that later we would return

Miss Gates's bankbook to her with an account of how we had spent her dollar. We knew that she would be gratified. I can't remember all we did, but, with a homemade lunch to save on food, we got ourselves to Golden Gate Park, saw the museums and art galleries, took in a ten-cent movie, and stretched the dollar to incredible lengths. The shame of it was that we never got around to writing it all out for Miss Gates's pleasure. We had such grandiose ideas of how cleverly it should be written and in what detail, that it never got written at all.

Someone told us that, if we went to the Campus Red Cross, they would give us free khaki-colored wool to knit sweaters for soldiers. It was true. They gave us the wool and we knit monstrous sweaters with many dropped stitches and sent them away to our favorite soldiers. No one had told us that we were supposed to take the finished product back to the Red Cross for distribution. For some time we were in a lot of trouble over that.

Miss Unwin kept us under her supervision for a respectable time and we felt very grateful to her. But then, one day, we went to her laboratory to call on her and she said, "Just a minute, girls, I'm dissecting a live rabbit and I don't want it to come out of the anesthetic." We were very tenderhearted where animals were concerned and we never went to see Miss Unwin again.

We were not completely irresponsible. We were both taking difficult courses and getting good grades in them. I remember that one of Nora's courses was paleontology. She had a deep curiosity about the past, the long, long past. I was allowed to go on a field trip with her class once, and I was delighted to see them digging odd little fossils out of the dry California cliffs. I have always thought that if I were to come back in another incarnation I would choose to be an archaeologist or some kind of digger into the past.

But what has remained longest with me of that year in Berkeley is the freedom we had, the long walks and talks that were never finished, the smell of ferry boats and the eucalyptus groves and the roses and the sea.

Nora came of an intellectual and an other-worldly family, and nobody had ever really told her the fundamental facts of life. I remember once that haltingly she admitted this to me and asked me what I knew. Haltingly I tried to instruct her, knowing very little myself.

We sat on a hillside looking out on the lights of San Francisco Bay, and there were crickets in the grass and the smell of eucalyptus over all. A very long time ago that was, of an age with the funny little fossils in the cliffs.

29

Little Victor

IT WAS FASHIONABLE in 1917 to give parties for soldiers. All kinds of organizations gave parties so that "our boys" might meet the right sort of girls. That our girls might not meet the right sort of boys never entered people's heads. Patriotism was all.

The good deaconesses of St. Margaret's Hall in Berkeley regularly gave such patriotic parties and afterwards we were accustomed to skirmishes in dark hallways with amorous representatives of the army or navy who were seeing the right girls home. But even in those days three years of coeducational college life prepared a girl for almost anything, and we knew how to put up our own defenses against the advances of the militia. Sometimes, however, we were a little disgusted. We liked to consider ourselves quite free, eager for the unexpected and the romantic. The trouble was that this was neither unexpected nor romantic. It was plainly a bore. And then Little Victor came into our lives. Oddly enough, Little Victor who said and did and expected nothing, turned out to be the unexpected and the romantic. We never got over the wonder of Little Victor. We used to sit up nights talking about him and bursting into delighted laughter.

Victor was really not little at all. He was well over six feet tall, broad-shouldered, and with frightful black eyebrows over wild black eyes. If we had spoken German, *lein* or *chen* might have served our purpose better than "little," for to us it was a term of endearment as well as a description. Victor's last name has been lost in the mists of time, but it was probably Smith or Jones or possibly Schmaltz.

It was at one of the St. Margaret patriotic parties that we first saw him. We were playing circle games for the benefit of those who did not dance, and perhaps the deaconesses had already discovered that this was a safer form of entertainment than the clutch of dancing where such inflammable material was concerned. We had been going around and around for some time with a great deal of patriotism and more or less merriment, when Nora and I made the simultaneous and amusing discovery that we had acquired an admirer.

This large, black-browed soldier always maneuvered himself into the circle beside one or the other of us. From the very start he was quite impartial, either one would do, and he seemed to know without being told that we belonged together. He arranged separately with each of the two of us to take her home. Individually we accepted. I don't know what he would have done if we had not been friends or lived in the same house. Some girls would have been angry, but we were perfectly enchanted. So the three of us walked home together, Victor in the middle with a girl on each arm. There was no skirmishing in the dark hall that night. Even the stoutest army man doesn't usually try to kiss a pair of girls goodnight in the same place at the same time.

I was solidly engaged that year and Nora was temporarily so, both of our men far away, and we welcomed Little Victor's absolute impartiality.

He was not very articulate and he seemed depressed. I think now it must have been the fact that we laughed so much that drew him to us. He needed cheering. We saw at once that he was not quite like the cocky college boys who were out for a lark and jauntily preparing to go overseas to have a great time "over there."

Before the evening was over we had most of Little Victor's story. He told it in detached bits with clumsy attempts at humor, but it was easy to sense the dark river of misery and apprehension underneath. The dull gleam of it looked out from the back of his eyes, even when he tried to laugh. He had been in the army for several years and he was sick of it.

"But why? How?" we asked. All the army men we knew had just enlisted, full of anticipation and exhilaration. We could hardly imagine that anyone had been in the army for years before the excitement of American participation in the war with Germany had started.

Victor's father had died when he was small and his mother had married again, a man he disliked who had treated him badly. I could understand that. At sixteen he ran away from school and from the mother whom he still idolized. He had looked eighteen and he lied to the recruiting officer about his age. They swore him in and shipped him to the Philippines. So he had stagnated in the Philippines for three years, with fever, boredom, drill under tropical suns, and nothing much to occupy his mind beyond the military routine. He was sick of it. He had thought of nothing but the relief of finishing his term of service and getting home to the life he had abandoned. But now, suddenly, after all that emptiness and boredom, the United States was in a war and he could not escape without deserting. All of this business about Germany—what did he know or care? His company had been ordered back from the Philippines, and for a few months they were training new recruits in Palo Alto and then they would be sent to France.

"To be killed," he said gloomily.

"But aren't you glad to see some action after all that boring time?"

"What for?" he asked.

"Why, for democracy, to make us safe, you know."

He really didn't know or care. The fine fire of the boys who were offering their bodies to enrich the fields of France had been burned out of him. He wanted only to get home to his mother. He was a little boy lost. We looked at him in wonder. We had never seen one like him before.

"It wouldn't be hard to desert," he said. "Lots of them get away." It was the second time that he had used the word one simply didn't say in those days.

"*Desert,* Victor? Oh, no, you wouldn't do that!" we cried in horror.

But he was in earnest, and something of the chill reality of soldiering struck us for the first time. Up to that point we had thought of war only in terms of glory, glory lit up by the splendid glow of a bursting shell. Apparently there was another side.

But we couldn't help coming back to laughter. War or no war, the world was a delightful place and we were alive in it. We sent Victor home laughing, and that was the last time we heard him talk of deserting.

After that he came for us every weekend when he had leave. He always had theater tickets or some place to take us. He hadn't known how to spend his pay, and his mother, who must have felt that she had failed him when he needed her, sent him additional money.

"These girls you meet on the street," he said, "they're buzzards. They don't want to be friends." So we became his friends. It was a beautiful arrangement for all three of us. He was generous and absolutely impartial, preserving from the first moment he saw us the most delicate balance of attention between us. He studied our likes and dislikes, and tried to indulge them as much as he could. His utter simplicity enchanted us. No bookish boy could have pleased us better that winter. When he brought us presents, we used to lecture him good-naturedly.

"Now, Victor, that's a foolish way to spend your money. Be a good boy and save it."

"But, gosh! What for?" he said. He used to bring us candy, two little boxes, exactly alike; and maybe he was laughing inside as fondly as we laughed at him. Most fellows had one girl. He had two. That was one up on the other guys.

At Christmas he gave us one large gift together. It was a magnificent blue and white toilet set. It was only one of a kind, too beautiful to duplicate. It contained one comb, one brush, one mirror, one soapbox, one of everything a girl would need. We laughed for a week over that, but never unkindly, I think. We divided up the items between us and loved Little Victor the more because he had supposed that two girls living in the same room would naturally share the same toilet articles.

After a play or a vaudeville show in San Francisco we would return on the ferry, leaning on the railing to watch the receding lights of the city, or sitting on the hard benches inside the ferry, Victor in the middle with a girl on either arm, and everybody happy.

At Easter he asked us to come down to Palo Alto and see the army camp. As I remember it, he came and personally escorted us. Nora and I stayed in the hotel, and Victor took us with pride to the company mess and introduced us to his friends. A soldier with two girl friends, one on each arm, and everybody laughing.

I don't know what the more sophisticated boys thought of Little Victor's strange arrangement, but then nobody was very sophisticated in those days. We weren't hard to look at, and maybe they even envied him. We made him go to church with us on Easter Sunday. We happened on a very tiny chapel full of flowers, and the fields around Palo Alto were all full of blooming yellow poppies and blue lupine. So where are the flowers of yesteryear? Progress has swallowed them along with the funny innocence of 1918. Now you may buy a wilted Easter lily from the florist for $15 including sales tax, and there is a housing project on the hillside where the poppies used to grow.

Victor knew that I was engaged and wearing a ring to prove it. About Nora he wasn't so sure. Just before his outfit was scheduled to leave, he manifested his first sign of differentiation between us. He took Nora aside one night and offered her a ring. It was not at all romantic, she said, and she gave him a gentle no. Perhaps he was relieved. Just the same, he took us both on a final date with no hard feelings toward anyone.

We hated to see him go. But he was happy and cocky now. He was ready to go to France after he had seen his mother on the way.

Writing was not one of his accomplishments and we never heard from him again. The war was over by November. I hope he made it safely home and found the right girl, and, yes, I hope he had two daughters, one for each arm, and maybe they would even use the same toilet set.

30

Our Babies

NORA AND I HAD made a school-girl pact to name our first daughters after one another. I was married the summer after I graduated from Berkeley. My first child was a boy.

Nora went back to the University of Idaho for her senior year, and, after graduation, she had a clerical job at the university. There she met a young professor of animal husbandry in the school of agriculture. She sent me his picture; he was tall and good looking. Even if he was not BH, we both knew that BH was a childish qualification and that now life was to be lived seriously.

He had a good teaching position, but he yearned for practical applications, so when the opportunity to manage a large Lamar-Duroc hog ranch in Texas was offered to him he accepted it with enthusiasm. Their honeymoon was the journey to Texas to the hog ranch.

It was a sudden transition for Nora from the gaiety and intellectual stimulus of a college campus to the flat monotony of a prairie ranch where she was the only woman for miles around. There were a couple of hired hands; she was the housekeeper and cook. "But how do you link sausages?" She had a lot to learn. She was in love, and she accepted what love gave her with her usual humor and philosophy. At first it must have seemed a great adventure.

Both of us busy, we wrote as often as we could. I was still in an academic setting, with books and lectures available. There were friendly people all around me and the excitement of watching the development of a little boy. When I found time, I wrote to her on the end of the ironing board while the iron was heating, or on the sink while the dishes were soaking. Nora replied with accounts of being up all night to assist with a difficult farrowing, and how cute the little pigs were when they came. She wrote about the funny old cowhand who did the chores and the long, long vistas of empty land and the terrible heat of the summer and the purple evenings when the heat lessened and the night full of the smell of alfalfa and clover.

"Oh, Caroline Sybil," she wrote, "there isn't a book within twenty miles, except for books on hog breeding and the very few I brought with me." I tried to send her things, but I was busy and we seemed to have years ahead of us. I loved to sit down with her letters, written in the loose, running hand, more careless and hurried now than it had been when she was writing papers on ancient civilizations or paleontology. To read her letters was like a visit, almost as good as the long walks and talks we had had in Berkeley.

Then there was the letter, full of shy delight, that told about the expected baby. "Now you must tell me everything, what clothes to make for it, what furniture to buy, what books I ought to read. Just now I feel so dreadfully sick and it's so hot, I haven't had the gumption to be properly elated."

She tried to be humorous about the bumbling country doctor who told her it was normal for a female in the family way to feel under the weather. But her legs swelled in the heat. There seemed to be no ending to the sickness. "Time will cure everything," she said. "Nine months and then we'll start to live again, and be so happy."

But toward the end she began to grow desperate. All she could think of was getting back to Idaho to be with her mother and in reach of a good hospital. Some women could farrow like the hogs on a bleak ranch in Texas, but something was wrong with her. She could not. She wrote me before they started their journey, still hopeful and amused—at least for my benefit. I did not know what to advise, to stay where she was or to risk the long journey? She felt that she must make it.

They had an old Model T Ford, and the roads in the early 1920s were rough, the lodging places few and far between. I received two postcards from her written on the way, in a hand more loose and careless than it had ever been, but always cheerful.

Premature labor pains overtook her in Kansas, and she died in a Manhattan hospital. The baby died too.

Nora's father, remembering in his own grief how close we had been, called me to tell me the news. I came from the telephone and sat down in a chair in the living room. My husband touched my hand, and did not try to force false consolation on me. Suddenly all the beautiful, bright colors had turned bleak gray. I sat there a long time. No tears, no tears, only the sound of closing doors, shutting away the boundless horizons of my youth.

During the next months I kept thinking that, if there were communication after death, the sympathy and understanding we had had should make it possible. If I went into a darkened room alone I would open my mind and heart, and say, "Nora, I am here." But no voice spoke.

Finally I had a very vivid dream. It was like the ascensions, painted by Renaissance artists, that I had seen in Italy and Spain. The whole sky in my dream was filled with concentric rings of color and light and figures clothed in luminosity going up and down. In the center of this splendor was my friend, and she leaned down to me to say that all was well and that I was to grieve no more. Whether this was a genuine revelation or only my subconscious mind trying to put a stop to an intolerable situation, I do not know. But after that I let her go.

One thing still bothers me sometimes. No one ever told me whether Nora's baby was a boy or a girl. But to know this seemed to me trivial and irrelevant beside the central fact of her death, so I never inquired.

Several years later, when our own baby girl was born, we named her Nora.

31

Blinky

O N A SEPTEMBER day in the year 1909 I was sitting in the parlor in my grandfather's big leather rocker that we used to call the Sleepy Hollow chair. One foot was curled under me, and my head was propped on my hand so that my hair fell over the side of my face as I read a book. The young man, who preserved this detailed picture and described it to me many times, did not notice the title of the book.

He was a very tall, dark-haired, dark-eyed young man who, at nineteen, with B. S. degrees in engineering and mathematics, had come to take his first job as a teacher in the prep school at the university. On one of his first days in a strange town, an older professor, an English teacher whom we all called Toppy, brought him around to our house. My grandmother rented one of the bedrooms that opened off from the parlor to Toppy, and it gave us a little sense of belonging to the outer world to have a man coming and going through our parlor.

The parlor would have been called a living room today. It was a large, high-ceilinged room that had been added to the old part of the house by my grandfather in one of his expansive moments. There were many bookcases, a piano, and a lot of odd, old-fashioned furniture. It had an outside door of its own that opened onto a porch festooned with climbing roses. The carpet in the parlor was a kind of faded apricot color with wreathes of indistinct white flowers woven into it. The wallpaper had never been changed since the room was built. It too was faded apricot. So there is the scene, and a thirteen-year-old girl is reading and scarcely looks up as the two men pass through to Toppy's room. Yet the young man always remembered.

He was a quiet young man who had progressed through school so rapidly and successfully that he had not had much time for frivolity. Because he was smart he was always a little too young for the social life of his classmates. Yet he had been president of the Hamiltonians, a fraternal debating society, at Kansas State College where his father was dean, and he had been captain of a ROTC company and had played Petruccio in a college production of *The Taming of the Shrew.* He was excellent at taming shrews on the stage, but he did not know very much about girls offstage. A very dear sister, about fourteen, had recently died a lingering and terrible death of pneumonia. Perhaps I reminded him a little bit of her.

His father had been a Baptist minister until the lack of privacy in a parsonage next to the church had driven a reticent and bookish man into the profession of teaching, where he could pursue his own interest in Shakespeare and the classics instead of worrying about other people's souls.

The family had moved from New York and New Jersey, where Raymond was born, to Michigan and Kansas. There were two other brothers, an older and a younger, and never much money, so it was good to get out of college young and begin to earn a livelihood as well as money for further education.

The first job offered him was at a high school in South Dakota. Raymond accepted it and began to make his plans, but then at the last moment the son of an old friend of the family who was a professor of Latin and Greek at the University of Idaho wrote, saying that there was a vacancy in mathematics at Idaho and why didn't Raymond try for it? He tried and got it. When he wrote asking to be released from the job in South Dakota the principal of the school replied that they would release him, but that such a fickle and unstable young man would never amount to anything in this world. How very nearly he missed going to Idaho!

Raymond always disliked his name. His mother, a pretty little blue-eyed woman with romantic ideas, named her second son Raymond Wellington Brink. The two resplendent names were actually family names, but the earlier recipients both turned out badly, and the second Brink boy would have preferred to be called John or Tom. When the third boy was born his mother had used up her grandest family names. She thought it all over and decided to name the newest son Wellington and change Raymond's middle name to Woodard for her grandmother Polly Woodard. So the young man who went to Idaho was finally named Raymond Woodard Brink. Toppy immediately nicknamed him "Blink" and to the rest of us he soon became Blinky.

I was dithering along in grammar school in those days, and I would still have been reading *The Little Colonel* books for recreation if Toppy had not made fun of them and put *Treasure Island* and *Kidnapped* into my hands. Actually we had a very good library, left by my father and my grandfather, and when I began to read good books for the first time I was entranced. Oh, the delight of discovering *Vanity Fair!* And then the teeming wealth of Dickens, which Aunt used to enjoy reading aloud. I was not much interested in boys.

We had what we called the Neighborhood Bunch at that time. It consisted of Gram and Aunt and myself, a few other young people and the family next door. They were a very amiable mother and father and three children. Beth, the eldest girl, was a sprightly beauty who bowled over masculine hearts including Toppy's. We used to get together about once a week at one of the neighborhood houses to play Flinch or Old Maid or Hearts. Toppy was bald and nearer my Aunt's age than ours, but he was an enthusiastic member of the Bunch and he taught us all sorts of guessing games and pseudo-magic. The new young man in town was Toppy's additional contribution to the jollity of the Bunch.

Blinky was soon on the best of terms with all of us. He and Toppy were great at inventing games and entertainments, and Bunch nights became our chief delights. Age meant nothing to us then. Toppy's bald head and Grandma's gray hairs were as essential to our fun as the tousled pates of any of the youngsters. Toppy and Blinky used to put on prodigious "mind reading" seances that kept us all guessing until we finally discovered that they had a complicated code of silent signals. And then the fun of being taken into partnership with one or the other to make a new code and mystify the others! There were charades and amateur theatricals.

On Thanksgiving, Gram and Aunt invited the Bunch to dinner. We girls helped with the serving, and I spilled cranberry sauce on the beautiful Mr. Brink and was terribly embarrassed. Between turkey and dessert the young folks all ran around the block to make room for the pumpkin and mincemeat pies. As we raced out the back door I caught the hem of my best silk dress on a corner of the wood box and tore off some yards of the lower part of my skirt. It was a day of tragic happenings but a day of great delight.

Toppy and Blinky disappeared over the Christmas holidays, and we suddenly noticed how much we missed them. Without them the Bunch lost its flavor. Christmas was always a lonely time for me, seeing my friends enveloped in the holiday family festival which was only complete with father, mother, brothers, and sisters. I ate too much candy, read too many books, was glad when school started again and the wanderers returned.

Toppy and Blinky spent as much of their free time at the house next door as they did at our house. I understood that I was only a little girl and that Beth had all the fatal attractions of the vivacious grownup. I accepted this wistfully and began to think that growing up might not be such a bore after all.

Blinky had a room across town and took his meals at a faculty dining club or at The Pleasant Home boarding house where, with meal tickets purchased by the month, one could get a delicious home-cooked dinner often including steak for twenty-five cents. A quarter meant something in Idaho in 1910.

From our watchtower window on the hill I often saw Blinky walking down Third Street on his way to the university. He walked very tall and straight, in a long gray overcoat and a dignified hat, trying to look as mature and experienced as some of his students.

In the snowy winters we used to spend much time coasting, bobsledding, or tobogganing. There was almost no skating, for the simple reason that we did not have a pond or river, and no one thought of flooding a vacant lot. But in the rare blue mountain air we toiled up the hillsides, dragging our sleds, for the exquisite pleasure of rushing down them again with scarves and mittens flying and yelps of delight.

One night Toppy and Blinky borrowed a bobsled and some of the younger members of the Bunch went coasting. My Aunt went along with us, whether as chaperone or for the fun, I'm not sure.

Eight or ten of us could ride in sardine proximity, our legs sticking out at the sides, on the long high sled with its two sets of runners. A well-packed bobsled could achieve great speed on the long snowy hillsides. Blinky was steering and we were going at full speed down an unfamiliar hill when suddenly a drop off yawned ahead of us and the only alternative was a board sidewalk with a fence on one side and the drop off on the other. Our town was full of these perilously constructed sidewalks like bridges over the gulfs and canyons of our rugged landscape.

It required a split-second decision and Blinky chose the sidewalk. We roared down it at terrific speed, the fence on one side, the chasm on the other. Life might have ended there in a crashing instant, and all the beautiful years ahead might have been lost. But we zoomed on down and made a perfect landing far below. There was only one casualty. My Aunt's leg on the fence side stuck out a little too far. The fence removed her stocking with the most delicate accuracy and never scratched her leg.

I think that was the moment when she began to dislike Blinky, while the rest of us were telling him what a superb steersman he was.

On Valentine's Day there came one of the biggest snowstorms of the year. The snow fell from early morning to late night in a white sheet. All our traffic, such as it was in those days, came to a halt. We were snowbound. On February 15 we dug ourselves out, and something very wonderful happened to me.

One of the first persons to get through was a boy from the florist shop with a bunch of pink carnations for me. Pink carnations in Idaho snow for a little girl who had just had a fourteenth birthday. It was simply incredible. There was a note and it said:

Little Dan Cupid had left on his way
To take you these flowers on Valentine's Day.
But the snow was so deep he could scarce make a track,
So in pity I beckoned the little chap back.

And besides—should I say it? Scarcely I dare
The poor little fellow's entirely bare.
And I feared if he trusted himself to the breeze
That in doing his duty poor Cupid would freeze.

As for me, I'm protected from all thought of cold,
For to send you these flowers my love's made me bold.
So take them please, Carol; my love's come to say
And pardon, I pray, this delay of a day.

My Aunt looked at these verses with a cranky eye. Of course, it could be considered a joke of some kind, flowers and talk of love from an old university professor who had just turned twenty to a child who had just turned fourteen. Well, surely no one took it seriously. I did. It wasn't the girl next door who interested him after all. It was me! To everyone else it was a charming episode – Lewis Carroll to Alice Liddell.

Along in late March or April the family with whom Blinky roomed experienced some kind of domestic crisis and he had to give up his room. While the university was in session most of the spare bedrooms in our small town were occupied. If you lost your room you were in trouble. Toppy came to Grandma and pled Blinky's case. He knew better than to go to Aunt. She was not only disgruntled with Blinky but she was very much annoyed with Toppy as well. One of Toppy's many amusements was the game *Truth*. This was a crude forerunner of group therapy. One evening Toppy and Aunt had played *Truth* and told exactly what they thought of each other. Now they were barely on speaking terms.

But Grandma said, yes, we could give Blinky the front spare bedroom that Leddy had once occupied and that usually was saved for Aunt Et and Uncle Ash, and he could have it until the end of the school year. So Blinky very gratefully moved in with us.

The Bunch went on playing together pretty much as always, although Toppy and Beth were unusually busy with college activities. I think that was the season when they played the leads in Shaw's *Arms and the Man* for one of the university dramatic clubs. Gradually it became more and more Blinky and me amusing ourselves in various juvenile ways.

He coached me in arithmetic for the eighth-grade state exams that terrified me. We would sit at the dining room table in the evening, working on problems, and, if I got a problem right, I was rewarded like a good little animal by a chocolate-covered nut. Aunt sat by with her fancy work to see that nothing shocking was said.

One of her friends had reported to her that her daughter who was in Blinky's geometry class said that Blinky used the letter "P" on his blackboard diagrams and she thought this quite indelicate, when there were so many less offensive letters in the alphabet.

I passed the exams and my horizons widened under Blinky's tutelage. He taught me to dance on the old apricot-colored carpet to the sound of waltzes and two-steps on the Edison phonograph with the blue morning-glory horn. Aunt sat by with her fancy work, and Blinky used to be polite, asking her to dance with him every other dance.

We began to invent elaborate codes of writing, numbers and symbols representing letters, so that, while it looked something like arithmetic, we could say shy and pleasant things to each other without having to take Aunt into our confidence. She saw to it that we were not often alone, but sometimes we went riding in the pony cart between the hedges of wild roses, and once we tried a huge "experiment" which was a first kiss for each of us.

Grandma liked the young man's phrenological bumps and she understood that girls of fourteen are no longer children, but Aunt saw with alarm that her "little darling" was slipping away from her. She was in a tizzy of apprehension. Before he left for the summer vacation, Blinky told her seriously that he intended to marry me when I was older and he had more to offer. She was perfectly furious.

That summer he sent me water lilies that he had gathered at the lake in Wisconsin where his family summered. He sealed the stems with wax and packed them in damp cotton; they came through beautifully. I had never seen white water lilies, only the tight, yellow button-like lilies that grew in our West. We wrote many letters. I watched for the postman. Years later I wrote a poem about a young girl with a letter who could have been me in those long summer vacation days.

The next fall I was a little older and everything was strange. Blinky went back to his old room. The Bunch fell apart and Aunt did not welcome Blinky to our house anymore. I had to hide my feelings about him to keep her in a good mood, and sometimes I wondered if she was right and if it was all a foolish dream. But sometimes we saw each other and had a few quiet words. His dark eyes had the same warm sparkle. Did he really mean what he had said to Aunt?

That year I was in prep school where Blinky taught a few classes, so he became Mr. Brink again. We passed each other in the halls with a nod and I did not distinguish myself in geometry. One of his jobs was coaching plays, and Beth was one of his star actresses in the university performances. It was decided that the prep school would put on *The Rivals* and somehow, although I was never good at acting, I got the part of Lydia Languish's cousin Julia. I think that Blinky had something to do with that, and, when the costumes arrived from the neighboring city, I had the two most beautiful gowns to wear. At the last moment the boy who was to play Sir Lucius O'Trigger fell sick. To save the play from disaster, Blinky stepped in and took the part himself. Sir Lucius was supposed to kiss Lucy the maid. After the first performance, it was whispered about among the cast that he *really* had. I did not like that at all, but I pretended to be unimpressed.

After the play the whole cast had a dinner party at the hotel. Somebody, probably my aunt, had told me that a nice girl never went to dinner at a hotel without wearing a hat, so I wore a hat. I was the only one who did. Nevertheless I had a very good time. I was glad to see that Blinky looked at me with the same kind of warmth in his nice brown eyes, even if he had kissed the maid in the play.

There was one notable Sunday afternoon when Aunt and Gram and I had been invited out to supper by the mother of the girl who was shocked by the letter "P." I could not stand either the girl or her mother, so I rebelled.

"I've got a theme to do. I simply can't go," I said.

It was rare for Gram to go out, but on this particular day they both went and left me to my theme. Many times in my childhood I was desperately lonely, but there were also times when I enjoyed my aloneness. This was one of them. To have the house to myself to think my own thoughts and follow my own pursuits—this was sweetened by the knowledge that I had escaped a boring visit with people I detested.

While I was savoring my aloneness the doorbell rang, and there stood Blinky. I had not called him. He had not seen Aunt and Gram depart. Some minor miracle had given us an afternoon together. I have no recollection of what we talked about, but all of the embarrassment of prep school classrooms and uneasy sessions with my aunt's hostility on the other side of the parlor disappeared. We were easy and friendly and it was a lovely afternoon, better than being alone.

Then I said that, if he would stay for supper, I would make clam soup. But I was so schooled in obedience and propriety, that, after he said he'd like to stay, I called up the folks to see if it would be all right. Fortunately Grandma came to the phone and she said that I might make clam soup for Mr. Brink. I was not a skilled cook, but I knew how to turn a can of minced clams and milk and butter and salt and pepper into a very tasty dish. We ate our first meal, alone together with jokes and friendship and complete happiness. It was a rare occasion that we always remembered.

The next year Blinky went away to Harvard. He had saved enough money to finance the rest of the education that he wanted. Now, although we were a continent apart, we were suddenly liberated and united in a very special way. We began to write letters, and in them we could say anything we wished: our thoughts, our hopes, our every day adventures, even sometimes (although they were not primarily love letters) a touch of love.

That year, for some reason that now appears to be obscure, Aunt and Gram and I rented the house and went to Portland, Oregon. There I spent my last two high school years in a private school called Portland Academy. I had intended to be a boarder at the school while Aunt and Gram lived in an apartment nearby. But I was overwhelmed by homesickness. Surrounded by young people who already knew each other and were easy and unselfconscious, I felt shy and strange. They did not need or welcome me, and I was more acutely alone than I had ever been in a silent, empty house. If I had had the gumption to stick it out for a few months I might have fitted myself in, but I turned tail and ran to the apartment where Aunt and Gram were living. I went to school in the daytime and returned to the old security at night. I kept a diary, and, like an old person, I lived very much in the past. Blinky's faithful letters meant everything to me.

My aunt broke her leg very badly that year. Both bones were broken and a steel plate had to be screwed to the bones to keep them from slipping past each other, making her a hopeless cripple. I am sure that they do those things better now, but it was a long time then before she walked again. We felt very sorry for her. It was a dreary year. I must have put much of my adolescent frustration and dreaming into my diary.

One of the lovely things in a bleak winter was that on Valentine's Day I received the usual bouquet of pink carnations from Blinky. Aunt was grimly silent about the carnations, as she had been about the letters which I received but did not share with her.

A few days after Valentine's Day, when I came home from school and opened my diary, there was a letter in it from Aunt. She asked me not to write to Blinky anymore, as he was not a fit person for me, and I was much too young to be involved with him. "Please don't speak to me about this, darling. Trust me that I know best."

I never forgave my aunt for that. I was sure that she had read my secret, secret diary, and perhaps my letters, and now she was asking me to give up one of the dear and human connections that I still had with the world. I don't know why I complied. She had dominated my life since I was eight years old and she was just struggling through a difficult disability. I felt sorry for her and helpless. A kind of numbness of defeat settled over me. I had experienced it at school, and now it descended even more terribly on me at home. I might have told Gram and probably she would have been on my side. There were several days when I did not know what in the world I was going to do. Then I wrote a letter to Blinky and said that I couldn't write to him anymore, and please don't ask me why and please don't write to me either, because it would just make things worse for me. No single word about the matter passed between Aunt and me, but I never wrote in my diary again. I think that year was the lowest spot in my life. I was just sixteen.

The next year Aunt and Gram stayed at home and I went back to Portland to finish my broken high school days at the academy. I stayed with friends who had girls near my own age. Life began to look brighter. I began to have fun again, and to like the taste of life. Only one thing was lacking. I needed the letters from Blinky.

One of the girls where I was staying got letters from a young man her parents didn't like through a loyal girlfriend. I could have written and received letters there perfectly well without my aunt knowing. But I had some sense of honor and obligation that I do not understand now that prevented me from doing anything behind Aunt's back without telling her.

I resolved to tell her, when I went home for Christmas vacation, that I was going to resume the correspondence with Blinky. My misplaced sense of honor is no more incredible to me today than my quiet belief that, when I wrote again, Blinky would be glad to hear from me. How did I know that in nearly a year of silence he hadn't married another girl or at least got himself engaged?

It was a miserable Christmas vacation. We had been silent on this subject for so long that I could not make myself speak of it, and yet I was determined that I must. Perhaps my difficulty was cowardice after all, and I didn't like to hurt people or to quarrel. I had to change trains in the middle of the night on my way back to Portland, and Aunt insisted on coming with me to the point where I changed to see that her "precious lamb" was safely on her way. We lay in a lower berth fully clothed for the first part of the journey, and I knew that it was now or never.

"Aunt," I said, "I'm going to write to Raymond again. I wanted to tell you before I did it, and please don't say anything to me. You'll have to trust me in this." So it was very easy once it came out. My sense of relief was so great that I can't remember what she said in return. No matter what she said, it was all right now. I had fulfilled my obligation, if there ever was one, by telling her. I was free. At last I was a responsible adult.

And just as I had imagined, he was delighted when I wrote to him, and there were pink carnations for Valentine's Day. The family I lived with was very much surprised.

"Whoever sent you those?"

"Well, I have a friend at Harvard."

"The one who writes to you?"

"Yes."

So they began to call him "the Harvard gink."

After that I went to college and had a wonderful time and got engaged temporarily twice, and "the Harvard gink" got a traveling fellowship to France and had a girl in Grenoble and a girl in Boston, but we never stopped writing letters and every Valentine's Day I had pink carnations.

One summer he came to Idaho to see me, but he didn't write to tell me he was coming because he was afraid that Aunt would prevent him seeing me if it were not done casually. As luck would have it, I was visiting a friend in southern Idaho. When he found where I was, he called me long distance, and it was arranged that he would come to see me there. But before he could come he received a telegram from the East which said that his father was dying. He had to go home as quickly as he could.

So it was letters again. We didn't see each other until he returned from France and I was starting my senior year of college at the University of California at Berkeley. Then he made a special trip to see me.

The war was going on, and, because of an eye difficulty, he was teaching soldiers instead of being one. His work at the University of Minnesota did not begin until late October, so we had a month of getting reacquainted, walking in the eucalyptus grove, eating seventy-five cent banquets with complimentary wine in San Francisco, and behaving like madcap children. My friend Nora was usually with us; she was not a hostile chaperone like my aunt. It was a lovely month. We understood that malevolent fate, familiarly known to us as "M Fate," had kept us apart long enough and that we would be married in the summer.

On my birthday eve in December, Nora and I sat up until midnight to open the package he had sent. It was a beautiful ring with three diamonds in a setting that he had designed himself. It was much more extravagant than he could afford, and usually he was thrifty. But at the same time he looked to the future, so now I have an heirloom ring to pass on to our daughter.

My aunt had married the year before, with, as I suppose one could expect after her long spinsterhood, no great feeling of congeniality. But I hoped that I might be married at her home or better still at Gram's old house where Gram still lived alone. I wanted only the simplest wedding with the few people I knew best near me, but I still yearned for the security of a family. I wrote to Aunt to this effect. She answered promptly that it would be quite impossible for me to be married at either her house or Gram's, that the best place would be to arrange a wedding at a hotel in Spokane.

That evening Nora and I had student tickets for a university concert by Schumann-Heink. At the last moment Nora could not find her ticket and I had to go alone. I sat, unseeing and unhearing, through a long concert. There was the final storm of applause and an encore. People began to leave the auditorium, but many were still standing and applauding. I was about to leave when the Diva came back again. I stopped and leaned against the wall near the door to hear the final number. She began to sing:

> Through pleasures and palaces though we may roam
> Be it ever so humble, there's no place like home.
> Home! Home! Sweet, sweet home. . . .

I rushed out into the California night, mild and smelling of eucalyptus and roses. I burst into violent tears. All the years of stoicism and acceptance of my lot washed away in a storm of self-pity. "I have never had a home," I said to myself, "never a home. What they gave me was always paid for out of the money my father left. Since my father's death I have never had a home."

This was not true, of course, in anything but a superficial sense; I never really ceased loving and being grateful to my grandmother and my aunt. In later years Aunt came to love and rely on Blinky, but at that time she was wildly angry with him. When she saw me off to be married in Wisconsin at the lake of the water lilies, she was the one to shed the tears. My face was turned toward the new life and I was happy to be done with the old. Perhaps it was better for me to have made a clear break and a new beginning so that I could give my whole heart to the mother-in-law who gave us a beautiful wedding under oak trees by the lake, to the new family, and to the husband whose tastes were always so near to mine. Was it because he "picked me young," as his brothers used to say, or because we naturally had the same bent of mind? We enjoyed the same jokes; we had the same work habits; we liked the outdoors and living in strange places; and we never got used to the wonder of the world. Because he said I was beautiful, I became beautiful; because I admired his strength, he was strong. We had a good marriage.

In these days of license and cynicism it is difficult to make young people understand about a marriage that begins with virginity and mutual respect as well as love and passion, and that in the end still keeps the love and mutual respect with the added blessing of a steady friendship. They do not understand that a really good marriage relationship between a man and a woman is the best thing that life can offer—better than a career or fame or money or any other relationship. It is not achieved without effort, patience, and an occasional bad day, but finally it is the one perfect accomplishment and joy the world offers.

In his last years a thought sometimes troubled him: that I might not remember him as he was when we were young, that I might think of him as an old man whose strength was beginning to be diminished.

But there was never any cause for anxiety. Dear friend, I remember.

Notes

1. Brink was born in Moscow, Idaho, in 1895. Her grandfather was William W. Watkins, her grandmother Caroline Woodhouse Watkins, and the aunt referred to here Elsie Watkins Phiel. Her father, an early town mayor, was Alexander Ryrie and her mother Henrietta Watkins Ryrie, who latter married Nat Brown. Unhappy in that relationship, she committed suicide. For additional biographical information, see the foreword.
2. The Ryrie house was located at 124 N. Polk and the Watkins house at 320 S. Van Buren Street. These and other addresses in these notes refer to 1990s street numbers.
3. The Watkins Medal for Oratory was the University of Idaho's first and — for several years — most prestigious award, given to the student deemed the most outstanding in an annual oratorical competition.
4. *Buffalo Coat* (New York: Macmillan, 1944; rprnt., Moscow, Ida.: Latah County Historical Society, 1980; rprnt., Pullman: Washington State University Press, 1993).
5. The Steffenses' home was at the northwest corner of White and Mountain View.
6. Brink received an honorary Doctor of Letters from the University of Idaho in 1965.
7. Tom Armour, Winnifred's son, was raised by his grandmother after his mother left her husband.
8. Members of the Industrial Workers of the World, or Wobblies, populated the fields and forests of Latah County, as they did in much of the American West prior to World War I.
9. Washington State College — now Washington State University — in Pullman, Washington.
10. William J. McConnell moved to Moscow in 1878 and became the town's leading merchant. He built the community's largest store on Main Street and in 1886 the house at 110 S. Adams Street that later became known as the McConnell Mansion, now operated as a museum by the Latah County Historical Society. McConnell served very briefly as a United States senator from Idaho and, from 1893-97, as the state's third governor.
11. Although some Moscowans believe the house took three years to build and cost $60,000, newspaper reports are quite clear that construction began in July 1886 and was completed in December that year. A figure of $6,000 is probably more accurate.

12. Mr. and Mrs. William Adair purchased the house after the McConnells left. The Adairs sold to Thomas Jackson, who sold to Frederic Church, who bequeathed the home to the county at his death in 1966.

Selected Bibliography

Works By Carol Ryrie Brink

*Denotes a work set in Idaho

Adult Fiction

*Buffalo Coat. New York: Macmillan, 1944; Moscow, Ida.: Latah County Historical Society, 1980; Pullman: Washington State University Press, 1993.
Stopover. New York: Macmillan, 1951.
The Headland. New York: Macmillan, 1955.
*Strangers in the Forest. New York: Macmillan, 1959; Pullman: Washington State University Press, 1993.
Château Saint Barnabé. New York: Macmillan, 1962.
*Snow in the River. New York: Macmillan, 1964; Pullman: Washington State University Press, 1993.
The Bellini Look. Des Plaines, Ill.: Bantam, 1976.
Rags and Patches. (Poetry). Self published, n. d.

Adult Non-fiction

Harps in the Wind. New York: Macmillan, 1947.
The Twin Cities. New York: Macmillan, 1961.
*Four Girls on a Homestead. Moscow, Ida.: Latah County Historical Society, 1978.
Camp: A Family Memoir. Santa Fe Springs, Cal.: Hunter Press, 1981.
*A Chain of Hands. Pullman: Washington State University Press, 1993.

Juvenile Literature

Anything Can Happen on the River. New York: Macmillan, 1934.
Caddie Woodlawn. New York: Macmillan, 1935.
Mademoiselle Misfortune. New York: Macmillan, 1936.
Baby Island. New York: Macmillan, 1937.
*All Over Town. New York: Macmillan, 1939.
Lad With a Whistle. New York: Macmillan, 1941.
Magical Melons. New York: Macmillan, 1944.
Caddie Woodlawn: A Play. New York: Macmillan, 1945.

Narcissa Whitman. New York: Row, 1945.
Minty et Compagnie. Dronten, The Netherlands: Casterman Nederland, 1945.
Lafayette. New York: Row, 1946.
Family Grandstand. New York: Viking, 1952.
The Highly Trained Dogs of Professor Petit. New York: Macmillan, 1953.
Family Sabbatical. New York: Viking, 1956.
The Pink Motel. New York: Macmillan, 1959.
Andy Buckram's Tin Men. New York: Macmillan, 1966.
Winter Cottage. New York: Macmillan, 1968.
*Two Are Better Than One. New York: Macmillan, 1968.
The Bad Times of Irma Baumlein. New York: Macmillan, 1972.
*Louly. New York: Macmillan, 1974.

Works About Carol Ryrie Brink

Brink, Carol. "Keep the Bough Green." *Horn Book* (1967): 447-53.
Oral history interview with Sam Schrager. Transcribed. In the library of the Latah County Historical Society. 1976.
Brink, Carol. "The Gold Mine of Experience." *The Writer* (Aug. 1977): 11-14.
Oral history interview with Mary E. Reed. Transcribed. In the library of the Latah County Historical Society. 1981.
Reed, Mary E. "Carol Ryrie Brink: Our Idaho Author." *Latah Legacy* (Latah County Historical Society). (Spring 1982): 1-9.
_____. "Folklore in Regional Literature: Carol Brink's *Buffalo Coat*." In Louie Attebery, ed., *Idaho Folklife: Homesteads to Headstones*. Salt Lake City: University of Utah Press and Boise: Idaho State Historical Society. 1985. 216-22.
_____. *Carol Ryrie Brink*. Western Writers Series no. 100. Boise: Boise State University, 1991.

Index